BOAT CANVAS

FROM COVER TO COVER
by Bob & Karen Lipe

How to Repair,
Maintain, Design
and
Make Canvas
For Your Boat

Written by Bob and Karen Lipe
Illustrated by Jim Kraft
Photography by Bob Lipe

Seven Seas Press 524 Thames St., Newport, RI 02840

Published by Seven Seas Press, Inc.
524 Thames Street
Newport, Rhode Island 02840

Book Trade Distribution by
Simon and Schuster
A Division of Simon & Schuster, Inc.
1230 Avenue of the Americas
New York, New York 10020

Manufactured in the United States of America
Printed by Kingsport Press
Bound by Kingsport Press

5   6   7   8   9   10   11   12

Library of Congress Catalog Card No. 87-062679

Publisher's ISBN: 0-915160-27-7

This book is dedicated to
our parents.

ACKNOWLEDGMENTS

For their help and encouragement we would like to
thank Steve Doherty, our publisher; Pete Smythe,
editor of *Motor Boat* Magazine; Emily Cook, our
typist and final proofreader, and Jim Kraft, the artist.
We deeply appreciate their help.

KSL & RWL
Fort Lauderdale, Florida
March, 1978

INTRODUCTION

We wrote this book to provide cruising people with clear and simple instructions for making "canvas work" for their boats. Doing your own canvas work is one of the crafts seamen have pursued for centuries, and, for the boat owner, it can provide real satisfaction. Not only does it reduce the cost of outfitting—which can be considerable for some items of custom canvas work—but it provides you with the type of canvas (or synthetic) "equipment" that exactly suits your cruising requirements and precisely fits your boat. The projects described here not only contribute to your comfort and safety aboard, but will, in many cases, protect your boat so as to reduce maintenance. More time and money saved for cruising.

While the projects laid out in this book have been designed and laid out primarily for sailboats, a considerable number of them are equally applicable to powerboats, especially powerboats that really cruise and anchor out and would benefit from added convenience and protection.

For the boat owner who is only generally interested in how canvas work is done, or who at best only makes an occasional repair when necessity requires it, there is much useful general information included. For example, this book should help you to select the most appropriate and durable fabrics even if you are having custom work done by a professional.

Toward this end, and to make the instructions easier to understand, we have included over 100 drawings and more than a dozen photographs. Before you begin any project, we strongly urge that you read the entire book. Get a feeling for the subject first. Most of the projects involve simple sewing techniques that are easy to master with a bit of practice, even if you've never done any sewing before. But it does take careful planning, lay-out, cutting and assembly to produce the kind of finished project you will be proud of.

Planning is the key to success. Go at it in steps: 1.) Decide on a project you need; 2.) List the required materials; 3.) Diagram your assembly parts; 4.) Purchase materials; 5.)Label all parts (include dimensions, reinforcement positions, etc.); 6.) Note special instructions that will help you visualize the steps and avoid errors; 7.) Then begin the work.

As this is a how-to book, you will be taken through each project step-by-step to completion. If you make a mistake or get tired, put it aside for the day until you are fresh and ready to go at it again. Remember the old carpenter's adage: "Measure twice, cut once."

Half of the success of your project lies in having the confidence to begin. Using the stages listed above, wade right in. After a few projects, when you have mastered the smaller skills used in any project, you'll probably find yourself trying your own projects.

Good Sewing!

Contents

LIST OF ILLUSTRATIONS

Chapter one

THE SEWING MACHINE

The projects in this book are designed to be sewn with a domestic sewing machine. Commercial machines will sew through more thicknesses at higher speed than a domestic machine. However, most of us do not require a fast machine, and most projects will not involve thicknesses a good domestic machine cannot sew through.

It should be noted, however, that a sewing machine is a complex mechanism. Care should be taken to keep the machine well oiled and in proper adjustment, especially when it is used to sew heavy fabrics. Many domestic machines sew lightweight fabric for years without being oiled properly, but we oil our machine faithfully every week because it is used from two to eight hours daily and almost always on heavy fabric.

An oiling diagram should be included in your machine manual. If not, get one from your dealer or manufacturer. Oiling may look complicated but it's simple enough if you approach it a step at a time. Start at the needle side of the machine and work to the right. Place a few drops of sewing machine oil in each oil port. The oil can be purchased from any sewing machine dealer. Be sure to run the machine sufficiently to work the oil into all moving parts. After oiling, run several rows of stitching on a scrap of material so if any oil escapes at first it will not soil good fabric.

Check the teeth in the pressure plate. After much use these teeth, which feed the material through the machine, may become dull and be less effective. Worn teeth can be replaced for a few dollars. Many machine models allow you to raise and lower these teeth. By raising them slightly higher than the normal sewing height, heavy fabrics will feed through more smoothly. Don't forget to lower the teeth again before sewing lighter fabrics.

TENSION

The upper tension and bobbin tension must be equally balanced when sewing or the stitches will not be strong and even. The bobbin tension is adjusted with a tiny screw on the bobbin case. This adjustment should only be made *after* the upper tension has been adjusted. The upper tension is adjusted with the knob on the tension wheel. Note your owner's manual. Proper stitch tension looks like Fig. 1-1.

When the upper tension is too loose, the stitches look like Fig. 1-2, and when the upper tension is too tight they look like Fig. 1-3.

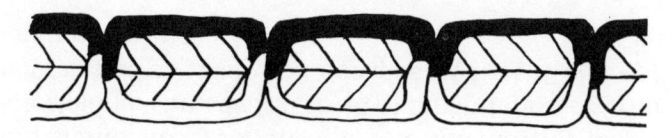

Fig. 1-1 *Proper Tension*

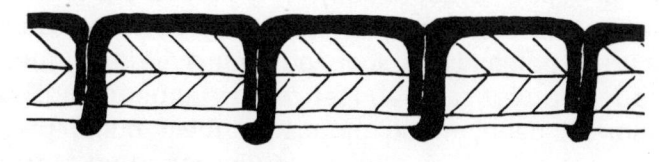

Fig. 1-2 *Upper Tension Loose*

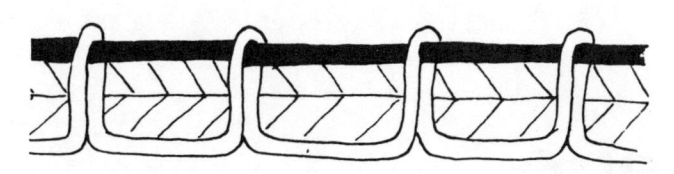

Fig. 1-3 *Upper Tension Tight*

Use patience in adjusting the tension. Trial and error is the only method. The stitch tension is important and may need changing with each different type of fabric you use.

NEEDLES AND THREAD

Heavy fabric should be sewn with number 16 or number 18 needles. The large needles pack more power and break less easily than small ones. They will also accommodate larger thread. We recommend the use of a good all-purpose polyester thread. It is strong, sun resistant and stretchable and will last longer out of doors than Dacron thread. You may try heavy-duty polyester thread if you like, but it will cause you more tension problems than the all-purpose thread.

Chapter two

CLOTH FOR VARIOUS PROJECTS

Choosing cloth for each project is an important consideration as the cloth will affect the project's longevity and esthetic value. Some materials are more easily sewn than others, and some are more easily folded and stowed. Thus, the entire project must be weighed against the individual properties of each fabric before choosing the best one for a particular job. We have taken the liberty of suggesting fabrics that we would choose for various projects and have listed the fabrics in order of preference. Another person skilled in the art of canvas construction might have other suggestions, and you might have your own ideas.

CANVAS

Traditional canvas is made of pure cotton thread and was, in the past, the exclusive material for sails, sail covers and seat covers. Today, however, we have many types of synthetic "canvas" which are grouped with cotton canvas as the weave, texture and various uses are similar.

UNTREATED CANVAS

Untreated canvas is soft, woven material that can be purchased in weights ranging from 8 to 24 oz. per square yard. The weight of the cloth will determine to a great extent the strength of the cloth as there are more threads per square foot in heavier cloth. There is, however, a limit to how heavy a material you can choose for certain projects. For instance, a sun canopy that is likely to be put up and taken down many times during a cruise cannot be easily stowed or handled if it is made of cloth heavier than 10 oz. However, a cover that is used for protecting the boat from ice and snow could be made of 13- to 18-oz. cloth, as it is usually only handled twice a year, is not stowed on the boat in most cases, and will withstand the forces of the wind much better than lighter canvas. It is worth noting that any canvas heavier than 13 oz. will be difficult for you to sew on a domestic machine. However, you will rarely need canvas any heavier than this.

You will find untreated canvas available in widths of 31" and 36" for general purposes, and as wide as 120" for covering decks or making large awnings. It retails for about $2.00 per yard for 31", 10-oz. canvas, and rises in price for greater width and heavier weight. The low price is the only reason for using untreated canvas when so many other materials are at hand today. It will mildew if allowed to get wet, will fade if dyed and is not particularly resistant to sunshine.

TREATED CANVAS

There are many brands of treated canvas some of the more popular being Vivatex, Graniteville, Terrasol, and Permasol. All of these are cotton canvas treated with a mildew-resistant coating. There is a small difference in price, but basically the difference between brands is in the colors available. Vivatex, the most well-known treated canvas, usually is to be had only in natural colors: pearl gray (which is really a pale green); colorless, which is a natural off-white with a slight brown fleck; and khaki, a golden tan. The traditionalist will probably choose one of these three colors: They used to be all that were available. Permasol and Graniteville come in a variety of colors and patterns and seem to hold up as well as Vivatex. Terresol comes only in natural colors. Treated canvas will last from five to seven years or more, with heavy use, provided it is kept reasonably dry and clean. We have covers made of Vivatex that are 15 years old and have had heavy use for the last six years. The cloth is still in good condition, but the stitching has needed replacing.

Treated canvas retails for $3.00 or $4.00 a yard. It usually comes in 31" and 36" widths and 8.98- and 10.38-oz. weights. Just a dollar more a yard, it is much superior to untreated canvas for most marine uses. It will shrink when wet, up to two percent of the cloth's original size. This usually has no affect on anything you make with it. However, when making something you wish to fit drum-tight at all times, you must allow for this shrinkage and make the item one percent larger than the required size.

SYNTHETIC "CANVAS" (Acrylic)

Yachtcrylic, as it is often called by distributors, is probably the best all-around material for boat covers, etc., when used outdoors. Its fibers are all acrylic and, therefore, will not mildew; it's quite resistant to the sun, and will resist fading fairly well. If the covers are well made they should last many years. Yachtcrylic comes in a standard weight of about 10 oz., and in three basic colors: bright blue, gold and white. Some companies offer a bright Kelly green, red and muted sea green; but blue, gold and white are most widely available. Acrylic awning fabric also is now being used in the marine field and is available in several stripe patterns. We have heard that this acrylic fades more readily than the blue, white and gold acrylic.

The only drawback to acrylic cloth seems to be its high price. A 39" wide yard will cost $5.00-$6.00.

It also has low resistance to chafe. Usually boat covers receive little chafe, but sacrificial patches must be sewn on the acrylic to save the outer material where chafing may occur. *Note:* Cotton canvas, untreated or treated, is the only *waterproof* fabric. Acrylic is very water resistant, but it may leak if a puddle of water is allowed to collect in it.

DACRON (Terylene)

Dacron is the synthetic fiber of which most modern sails are made. It is tremendously strong and water resistant. It also resists mildew well but is very susceptible to damage by sunlight. Some people recommend making awnings of lightweight Dacron. We would *suggest* making only sails of it and keeping them covered at all possible times! Dacron rots quickly in the sun and does not make a good awning or anything else that must remain in the sun. It comes in varying widths and runs from $2.50 to $6.00 a yard, depending on weight.

SPINNAKER CLOTH OR NYLON SAIL CLOTH

Nylon is somewhat less susceptible to the sun's rays than Dacron, but it will stretch where Dacron will not. It is very light weight and therefore many people will choose it to make sail bags, ditty bags and awnings. That is all right if you reinforce the strain positions well and don't mind the incessant crinkling noise that it makes in the wind. Nylon is the most difficult of all woven cover materials to sew on as it is slippery and tends to slide around when being sewn. Neither Dacron nor nylon breathes as well as canvas does. Nylon sells for $3.00 to $5.00 per yard and comes in various widths and colors.

WEBLON

Weblon is a Dacron-reinforced vinyl laminate material. It is either a heavy laminate of vinyl, or it is vinyl laminated to Dacron fabric. Many of the Bimini tops and weather cloths you see on power yachts are made of this material. It is waterproof but it does not breathe. Do not cover anything with Weblon that can be damaged by condensation . It is washable and has a fine texture resembling window screen. When laminated to cloth, several different color combinations are available as well as floral patterns and stripes. Weblon Hi-Tear (vinyl laminate without cloth backing) will stretch. If water is allowed to sit in a Weblon cover or awning, a permanent depression may form from the weight of the water. Weblon is quite difficult to handle while sewing pieces of it together. It resists bending and molding, so think twice before using it to make a cover with much curve to it. Weblon sells for around $6.00 per yard depending on pattern, and comes in 31" and 60" widths at 11 oz. per linear yard.

UPHOLSTERY FABRICS

Herculon is a polypropylene fiber woven in a variety of solid, plaid, floral and tweed patterns. There is a latex coating on the back of it that makes it water resistant and quite stable. It is also treated with a waterproof coating that will work for a while. It is used often for interior cushions on boats and trailers and, when new, is fairly resistant to stain. It is also quite difficult to sew as the rubber-type backing sometimes creates a drag on the machine. A bit of CRC (a silicone lubricant found in most hardware stores) sprayed on the seam line as you sew will enable the cloth to slide more smoothly through the machine and will not harm or stain the cloth. Many fabric stores sell Herculon for considerably less than the upholsterers do. It should sell for about $4.00 to $6.00 a yard in a fabric store or between $10.00 and $12.00 at an upholstery shop. When making cushions with this fabric, make the cover ½" smaller than the cushion as the fabric will stretch a bit.

There is also a new fabric on the market that resembles Herculon. Its fibers, however, are nylon backed with latex. It is comparable in every other way to Herculon.

VINYL

Good vinyl has a heavy but soft and flexible backing that gives it a spongy feeling. Naugahyde has a very fine reputation as it is usually excellent cloth, but there are others that are as well made that you may never have heard of. Beware of vinyl that has a thin "cheeseclothy" backing. It will tear easily and will not provide that leatherlike feel or comfort. Vinyl has been used often for interior cushions as it is resistant to water, milk, etc., and is easily cleaned off with a wet sponge. Its tendency to stick to the skin after you've sat on it for a while in the heat is a major drawback. It is the most maintenance-free material for cushions, however. When sewing vinyl, care must be taken not to make too many needle holes as these will make it tear eventually.

CANVAS FOR CUSHIONS

Canvas, as described earlier, has the soft nonsticky qualities that vinyl and Herculon lack. It is waterproof but not stain resistant. It can be washed and dried easily in the washing machine and dryer providing *you preshrink the material before making up the cushions.* It is easily handled in the sewing machine and provides a homey atmosphere and an easy change of decor. Canvas cushions will have to be replaced much sooner than Herculon or vinyl cushions.

OTHER FABRICS FOR UPHOLSTERY WORK

Corduroy and cotton/polyester blends of fabric make attractive upholstery. Obviously, you must consider the wear and tear they will receive, the water and food stains they may suffer, and the upkeep they will require. The only fabrics that are not suitable for upholstery are the linenlike fabrics with very loose weave. These will stretch in no time and give a very loose, sloppy-looking fit. Most fabrics can be waterproofed to some extent, but don't forget the old enemy mildew. A damp cushion can make a whole cabin smell musty.

Knits and other stretch fabrics are bad choices for upholstery and draperies. They will stretch and the threads will pull with the slightest rough treatment or heavy usage.

DRAPERY MATERIALS

Any synthetic or synthetic/cotton blend will make good draperies. The more wash-and-wear they are, the better. Definitely line them with a synthetic material if lining is necessary. Design and pattern are very important to good-looking draperies. They will be discussed in a later chapter.

CLOTH CHART

Fabric	Width (in inches)	Water-repellant	Water-proof	Stretchable	Rots in sunlight	Mildew resistant
Canvas	31, 36, 42	Yes	Yes	2%	Yes	No
Treated Canvas	31, 36, 42	Yes	Yes	2%	In time	Yes
Yachtcrylic	31, 41	Yes	Yes	No	Eventually	Yes
Dacron	31, 45	Yes	No	No	Yes, quickly	Yes
Nylon	36, 45	Yes	No	Yes	In time	Yes
Spinnaker Cloth	40	Yes	No	Yes	In time	Yes
Weblon	36, 60	Yes	Yes	Yes	Eventually	Yes
Herculon	54	Yes	No	Yes	—	Yes
Cotton/Poly	45, 54	No	No	No	Yes	No

Chapter three

TOOLS FOR CANVAS WORK

Descriptions of tools pictured in Photo 3-1 are as follows:

Scissors should be sharp and made of good steel or aluminum. Cloth edges that are cut well provide easier sewing.

Ripper used for ripping out mistakes, should be sharp and it should be respected. Used properly, it will rip a seam nicely in a short time. If used carelessly, it will rip material and skin.

Measuring tape and yard stick should be employed before cutting the cloth. A good design, well cut out, will make the sewing simple.

Grommet tool and die will be needed for setting grommets, and can be purchased at good hardware or marine stores. Each setter fits only one size grommet. Numbers two and three are good all-around grommet sizes. Both sets include a hole cutter, base die and grommet setter. Cut a hole wherever required in the material with the hole cutter and a hammer. Do not cut the cloth on a hard surface as the cutting edge of the hole cutter will chip and dull. Use a piece of hard wood or lead as a "backing block."

Place the male half of the grommet, flange down, on the base die. Place the hole in the cloth over the male end of this grommet. Put the female half of the

11

grommet over the cloth. Center the grommet setter in the hole of the base die and tap the setter lightly with the hammer. Increase the strength of your hammer blows until the grommet is set. If the grommet can be twisted in the cloth, it is too loose. Repeat setting procedure if necessary.

Plain grommets work well on two to four thicknesses of canvas, and spur grommets work better when more layers are involved. The small setter and die is usually found in a grommet kit and will not last very long. For putting in a few or a dozen grommets, though, a kit is sufficient. The procedure is the same as above.

Photo 3-1 *Necessary Tools*

12

Snap setter of the small-setter type is found in snap kits made by Dot Fasteners. A hole should be made with a ripper, leather punch or nail and then the male end of the snap, often looking like a button, is placed on the rubber disk. Place the hole in the fabric over the male post of the snap. The female top (or bottom) of the snap is placed on top of the fabric and male fitting. A spool of thread can be used to set the snap if you do not have the dowel shown. More efficient snap setters are available such as the vice-grip set shown. However, the vice-grip set retails for about $30.00 (and is usually not worth the investment unless you know you are going to do a great deal of snap setting).

Photo 3-2 *Cutting the Hole*

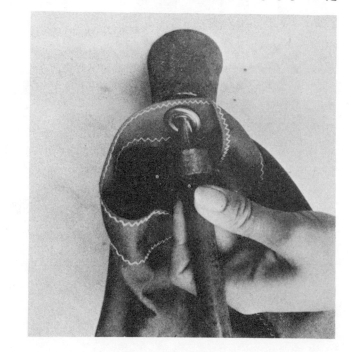

Photo 3-3 Setting the Grommet

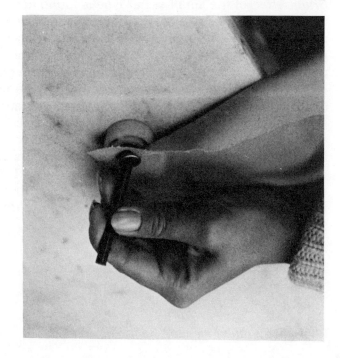

Photo 3-4 Setting the Snap

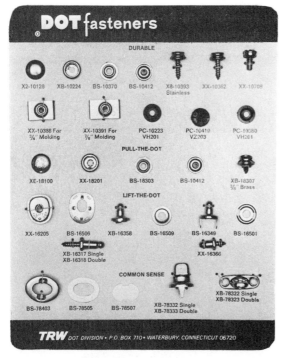

Photo 3-5 *Fasteners*

Fasteners shown in Photo 3-5 are the types of snaps and grommets available and most often used. Dot Fasteners manufactures the majority of them and they are sold by most marine hardware stores. Twist fasteners don't mix well with salt water as they may foul and become unturnable. However, if there will be considerable strain on the fastening, a snap will not hold. If you do not wish to use grommets and lacing, the twist fastener is another alternative. It can be easily installed with a pair of pliers. The various snap fittings shown in Photo 3-5 should be used for their designed uses. There are a number of possible combinations available to fit each situation.

15

Chapter four

SEWING TECHNIQUES

USING THE SEWING MACHINE

For success in canvas work, you should be familiar with the sewing machine you are using. If you are not, practice on scraps of cloth with this manual in hand. Learn what each knob and lever on the machine does. Here are a few universal terms that will help:

Tension as discussed in Chapter 1, is most important. It is controlled by the upper tension knob and a screw on the bobbin case. If the material doesn't feed smoothly, skips stitches, or if stitches are loose (as described in Chapter 1), adjust the tension. Always adjust tension with the presser foot down.

Pressure is created by the presser foot. This foot holds the fabric firmly while the machine is stitching. Regulate the pressure so that material feeds smoothly. It is too tight if the fabric puckers or drags or is too thick to go under the foot; too loose if the fabric slips or stops feeding.

Backstitching is usually done with a reverse lever or knob. This is a method of locking the stitching so that it will not unravel at the beginning or end of each seam. You should lock all your seams at the beginning and end by this method. If your machine

17

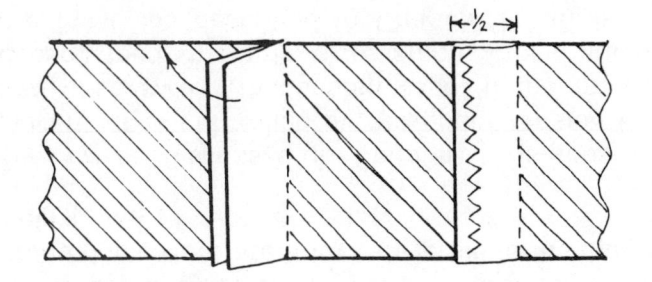

Fig. 4-1 *Finishing Seams with Zigzag*

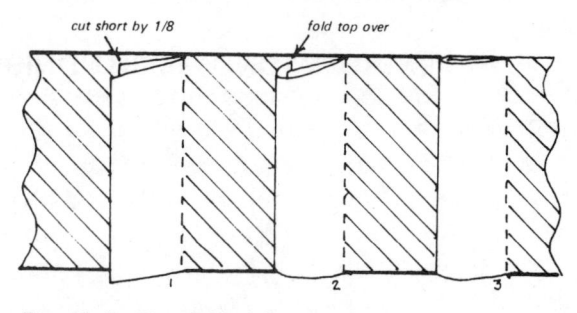

cut short by 1/8   fold top over

Fig. 4-2 *Flat-felled Seams*

has no reverse, stitch an inch at the beginning of the seam, rotate the needle to its up position with the hand wheel, raise the presser foot, move the material to its beginning postion and stitch again over the first stitching.

Seam is made when you sew two or more pieces of fabric together.

Seam allowance is the amount of fabric allowed between the stitching line and the edge of the material. In all of the following chapters a one-half-inch seam allowance is given and recommended. Seam allowance can be finished by zigzagging it to the underside of the material, (Fig 4-1), or by making a flat felled seam. (Fig. 4-2)

Pin Basting is done by placing pins perpendicular to the seam line to hold pieces of cloth together while stitching them.

Darting is a method of removing a triangular area of cloth, called a dart, without cutting away the material. It is most often used in canvas work to take the fullness out of hems or to remove excess cloth in covers. Begin stitching at the widest end of the dart and taper the stitching down to zero so that the dart will lie flat.

Hem is the finished edge. One should allow for 1½" to 2" of material for hems. Selvage edges, (the factory-bound edge of the material), can be turned up the allowed hem allowance and stitched. (Fig. 4-4) However, raw edges that will ravel should be turned under ¼" and then turned under again 1¼" or 1¾" to finish the hem. (Fig. 4-5) Since most fastenings, like grommets and snaps, are mounted in the hem area, it is important to leave enough width in the hem to accommodate the fastener. If no fastener is needed, hems can be narrower.

Casing is like a hem only the two ends are left open to receive a batten, length of line, shock cord, or curtain rod.

Stitching a Seam From Start To Finish
Thread your machine. Turn the hand wheel to raise the needle to its highest point so that the thread will not slip out of the needle as stitching starts. (This should always be done at the end of every seam to prevent knotting on the underside of the material.) Draw needle and bobbin thread under raised

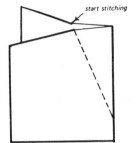

Fig. 4-3 *Darts*

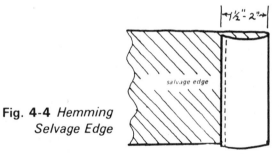

Fig. 4-4 *Hemming Selvage Edge*

19

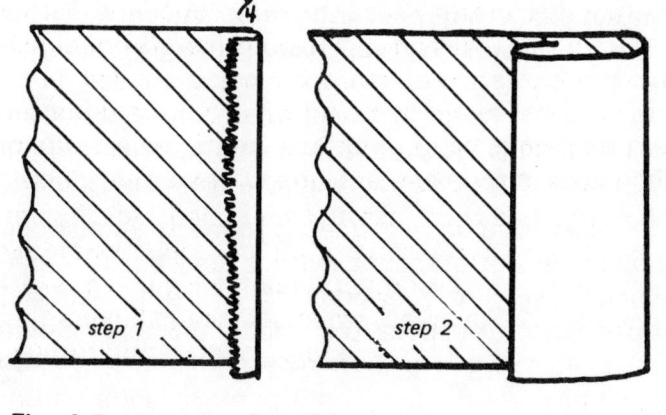

Fig. 4-5 *Hemming Raw Edge*

presser foot. Place fabric under raised presser foot with the seam edge on the right, and the bulk of the fabric on the left of the needle. Enough fabric should lie on the machine to prevent dragging. Lower the presser foot.

Start the machine with the foot pedal or knee lever. (You may have to turn the hand wheel a quarter turn to get the machine started.) Stitch an inch and then backstitch an inch. Run the machine at an even speed, reducing speed as you come to the end of the seam. Backstitch an inch. Stop the machine. Raise the needle to its highest point, lift the presser foot, draw out the fabric four or five inches from the needle and clip the thread (top and bottom) with scissors close to the fabric.

Guiding The Fabric

Most material can be directed under the needle by holding it with both hands in front of the presser foot. Heavy material and very light material may require the right hand to be behind the presser foot to guide the material, and the left hand to be in front of the presser foot. Heavy or slippery fabrics may require light pulling to help the feeder move the cloth through. You must coordinate this gentle pulling with the speed you are running the needle. If you begin breaking needles or enlarging stitches you are pulling the material too hard. Breaking needles continuously will damage the pressure plate on your machine. For very thick layers of canvas you may have to make the first few stitches by rotating the hand wheel with your right hand.

Reinforcing Stress Points

Reinforcing stress points can be done in a number of ways. The most common method is the extra patch. Wherever there will be a stress point, sew a small patch over that point. Stress may be caused by strain from weight, wind or stretching when the item is in use. Since your grommets should only be placed in two or more layers of cloth, (such as in a hem), place a patch 1¼ times the size of the grommet wherever a grommet is to be set in less than two layers of fabric. If extra heavy strain will be applied, as happens at the corner of a winter awning, several patches of differing sizes should be sewn, one on top of another. (Fig. 4-6)

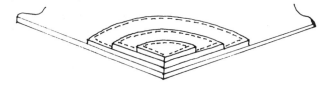

Fig. 4-6 *Reinforcing a Corner*

21

Reinforcing Slashes Or Cutouts

When a slash or cutout must be made to accommodate any protrusions such as shrouds, stanchions, cleats, masts, etc., the reinforcement patch can also finish the raw edge of the cloth. Cut a patch 1½ times the length and width of the slash or cutout. Pin this patch to the right side of the material. Draw the desired slash or cutout on the patch. Stitch along the drawn line for a cutout and to the sides of the line for a slash. (Fig. 4-7, Fig. 4-8) Cut between the stitching, taking out as much of the unnecessary

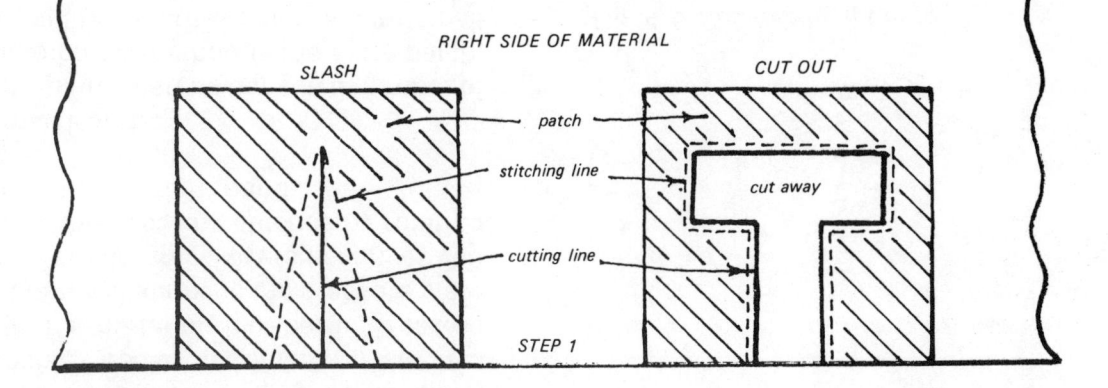

RIGHT SIDE OF MATERIAL

SLASH

CUT OUT

patch

stitching line

cut away

cutting line

STEP 1

Fig. 4-7 *Slash*

Fig. 4-8 *Cutout*

cloth as possible. However, don't cut any closer than ⅛" from the stitching. In the corners, cut diagonally right up to the stitching. Turn the patch to the inside and work out all wrinkles.

If the cloth pulls, you have not clipped the corners close enough. On the outside, topstitch (stitch on the right side of the fabric close to the seam) (Fig. 4-9) around the edge of the slash or cutout.

On the inside, fold under the raw edges of the patch and stitch to the main piece of cloth. (Fig.4-10)

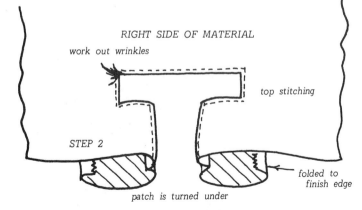

RIGHT SIDE OF MATERIAL

work out wrinkles

top stitching

STEP 2

patch is turned under

folded to finish edge

Fig. 4-9 *Turn Patch and Topstitch*

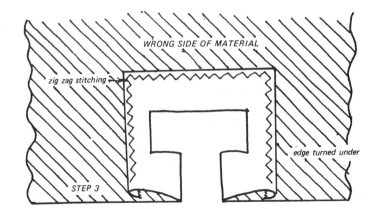

WRONG SIDE OF MATERIAL

zig zag stitching

edge turned under

STEP 3

Fig. 4-10 *Hemming Reinforcing Patch*

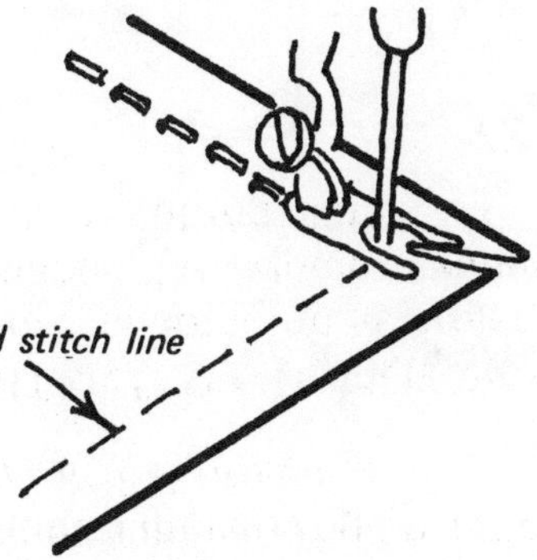

slash almost to needle

intended stitch line

Fig. 4-11 *Making a Corner*

Turning Corners

Whenever you must turn a corner, follow this procedure. Stitch up to the corner. Rotate needle through the fabric exactly at the corner. Slash the seam allowance almost to the needle. Lift the presser foot and rotate the cloth 90 degrees. Lower the presser foot and begin stitching again. (Fig. 4-11)

To make a gradual curve, make several slashes in the seam allowance of the fabric as you stitch the curve. (Fig. 4-12)

Right Side vs. Wrong Side

Often we will refer to the "right" or "wrong" side of the material. Canvas cloth does not usually have a right and a wrong side to it. The right and wrong side in this case is decided by the side you choose to turn the hems, place the seam allowance, etc. As long as you are consistent throughout the project, right side and wrong side won't be confusing, but *every* time you begin to sew a seam or hem be sure to *check* the material to make sure you are not switching sides.

AUTHOR'S NOTE: As you will be using these techniques again and again, practice them before you begin your first project.

IMPORTANT: We strongly urge the reader to read the *entire* chapter on a project *before* starting it. Understand the whole sequence before buying materials or cutting cloth.

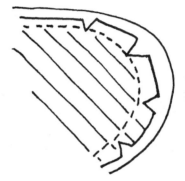

*two pieces of material
only one is curved
the other is straight
slash the straight piece*

Fig. 4-12 *Stitching a Curve*

Chapter five

MAKING A CANVAS BUCKET, DITTY BAG OR RIGGER'S BAG

The ditty bag, a favorite of sailors since square-rigger days, is a cylindrical bag made of cloth, and has literally hundreds of uses. A simple ditty bag with drawstring closure will conveniently hold anything from clothespins to spare parts. Make it larger, and you have a sail or laundry bag. Put a metal or wooden hoop in the top and give it a rope handle, and you have a rigger's bag that will not only stand up by itself, but also carry various rigger's tools when someone has to go aloft. It will also serve as a canvas bucket.

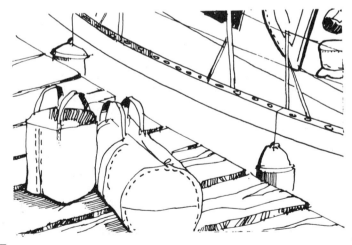

27

MATERIALS NEEDED

Canvas
(Vivatex, Yachtcrylic, Permasol, Spinnaker Cloth or Sailcloth)

Polyester Thread

For Ditty or Sail Bag: Length of line to match the circumference plus four inches.
1 or 2 grommets

For Canvas Bucket: Wooden, metal or plastic hoop to match the circumference of the bucket.
4 grommets
6 feet of ½" line for handle

For Rigger's Bag: 1 circular piece of ¼" or ⅛" plywood, cut to the desired circumference of the bottom of the bag.
1 length of ⅛" line for drawstring, if required
2 grommets
6 feet of ½" line for handle

ASSEMBLY INSTRUCTIONS

Step 1. Decide upon the size of bag you need. An "average" ditty bag might have a diameter of 5" and a height of 8". A rigger's bag should be larger, say 10" in diameter and 15" high. Select the size that suits your purposes.

Step 2. Cut two circular pieces of canvas the diameter of the bag. This can be easily done with a ruler. For instance, if the diameter is 10", place the ruler on the cloth. Mark the center at 5" and the limits of the diameter at 0" and 10". Rotate the ruler keeping the center mark at 5" and continue to mark the outer edges at 0" and 10" (Fig. 5-1). This should give you an accurate circle for the finished size. Now, remember that you must have ½" seam allowance. Place the center mark at 5½" and the limits of the diameter at 0" and 11", mark as before. This will give you your cutting line.

For small ditty bags, one circle is sufficient. For bags that will carry heavier gear, cut another circle to match the first, to make a double bottom.

28

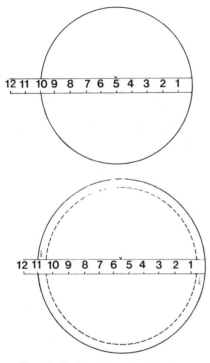

Fig. 5-1 *Marking A Circle*

Step 3. Figure the circumference of the circle by multiplying the diameter of the circle by *pi* (3.14):

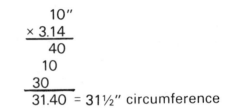

$$\begin{array}{r} 10'' \\ \times\,3.14 \\ \hline 40 \\ 10 \\ \underline{30} \\ 31.40 \end{array} = 31\frac{1}{2}'' \text{ circumference}$$

Step 4. Add ½″ at each end for seam allowance to the circumference for the total length measurement of the main piece of cloth.

(31½″ + 1″ = 32½″)

Step 5. Decide on the height of the bag. Add 1½″ for the hem and ½″ for the seam allowance at the bottom.

(15″ + 1½″ + ½″ = 17″)

Step 6. Cut the main piece of cloth. Our example will have a height of 17″ and a length of 32½″.

29

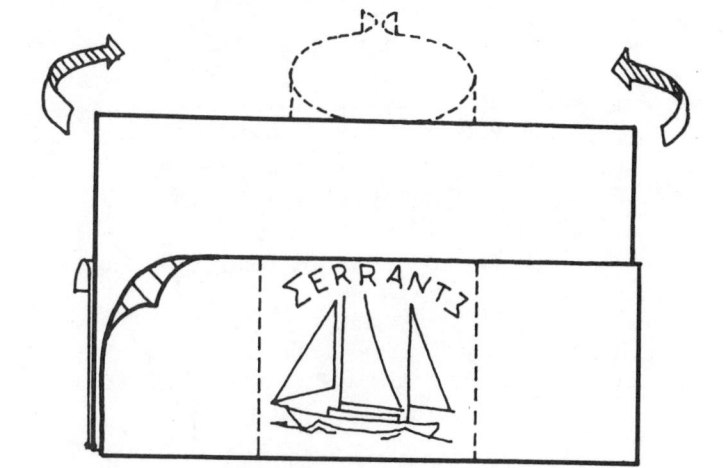

Fig. 5-2 *Layout of Pockets*

Step 7. If pockets are desired, cut one or two more strips of cloth to be sewn onto the main piece for pockets. The length should be the same as the main piece and the height a bit over half the height of the bag. For the example bag, the pocket strips should be cut 32½″ × 8″. Don't forget to add ½″ for the hem on the top of the pocket strip and ½″ for the bottom seam allowance. If you wish to make pockets on the inside *and* the outside, hem the top edge of each pocket strip and pin the two pocket strips to the main piece, one on each side. Line up the bottom edges of all three pieces and sew vertical lines of stitching to create pockets. If only one strip of pockets on either side of the main piece is required, follow the same procedure using only one strip of cloth. Reinforce the pockets by stitching over the first stitching twice more. If you wish to add a design done with embroidery, ink, paint or cloth on one of the pockets, do the design before sewing the pocket strip to the main piece. (Fig. 5-2)

Step 8. Fold the main piece of cloth in half, right sides together, forming the side seam. Stitch this seam ½″ from the edge of the cloth. (Fig. 5-3)

Step 9. If two thicknesses of bottom will be used, stitch the two bottoms together, close to the edge of the material.

Step 10. Place the bottom piece in the bottom of the main piece, right sides together. Pin the bottom in place with the pins perpendicular to the seam line (Fig. 5-3). The sewing machine needle will sew over pins that are placed perpendicular to it, but will have difficulty sewing over pins placed parallel to the seam line.

Step 11. Sew the bottom in place by stitching ½" from the edge of the material. Reinforce this seam by stitching again. Zigzag the edge of the bottom if possible. Turn the bag right side out.

Step 12. Place the drawstring grommets. In a small bag, where small line will be used, one grommet is sufficient. In a heavier bag, distribute the weight evenly by using two grommets on each side.

Ditty or Sail Bag

Set the grommets 1" in from the top edge. Stitch down 1¼" of material as in a hem. Put the drawstring

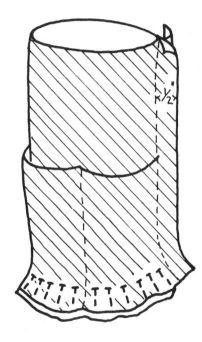

Fig. 5-3 *Stitching the Side Seam*

31

through the grommet or grommets and roll the material over it to make the hem and line casing. Stitch the hem down, being careful not to catch the line with the needle. (Fig. 5-4)

Rigger's Bag or Bucket
Fold ½" of cloth down around the top edge and stitch. Fold a 1" hem down around top edge and stitch. Set grommets through both thicknesses of cloth in the

hem area. (Fig. 5-4) If extra heavy gear is to be carried, reinforce the grommets by placing an extra patch of material under the grommet before setting it. Splice on rope handles as you choose or knot them as shown in Fig. 5-5.

Rigger's Bag Cut plywood bottom the exact circumference of the bottom of the bag. Sand rough edges and place in the bag.

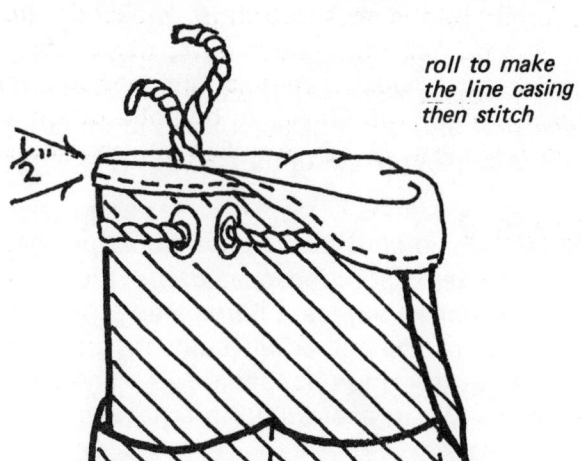

roll to make the line casing then stitch

Fig. 5-4 *Rolling the Line Casing*

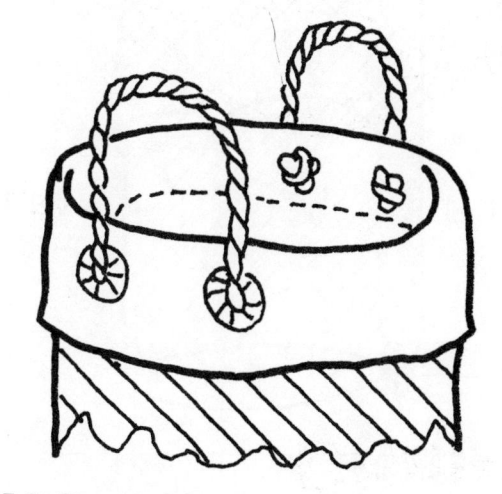

Fig. 5-5 *Rigger's Bag*

Chapter six

A SIMPLE DUFFEL BAG

This simple duffel bag is a handy traveling companion or storage bag for diving gear, laundry, out-of-season or specialty clothes or special equipment. The design given here is plain but can be customized with pockets, different straps and materials to fit your needs.

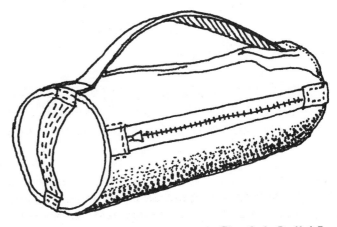

Fig. 6-1 *Duffel Bag*

33

Suitable Materials

Yachtcrylic   Spinnaker Cloth
Treated Canvas   Heavy Cotton Duck

Necessary Materials

A piece of cloth large enough to make the duffel (refer to the cloth chart in Chapter 2 for cloth width)

For the simple duffel:
1 piece of cloth 32" × 37" for main piece
2 circles 10" in diameter for the two ends
1 strip of cloth 4" × 38" for a long handle
1 strip of cloth 4" × 11" for a short handle
1 zipper 34" long, preferably heavy duty Delrin 5-D
2 spools polyester thread

Assembly Instructions

Step 1. Cut material to above measurements or to satisfy your own size requirements. Remember, extra cloth is needed for pockets and don't forget to allow for ½" seams.

Step 2. Handles: Fold each handle strip in half lengthwise, right sides together. Stitch ¼" from raw edge of material and across one end of each handle. (Fig. 6-2)

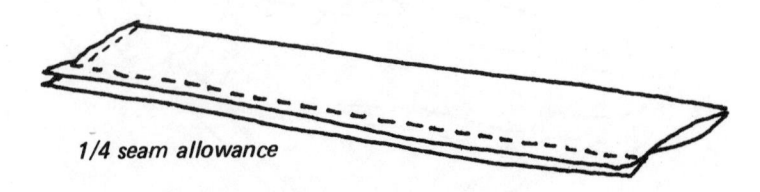

1/4 seam allowance

Fig. 6-2 *Handle*

Turn inside out by placing the eraser end of a pencil or a small dowel rod against the sewn end of each handle. Roll the cloth down over the pencil until the sewn end works its way out the open end. Pull on the sewn end or shake the handle so that it turns completely right side out. Topstitch the handle strips with four equally spaced rows of stitching.

Step 3. Top End: Lay short handle across one circular piece of cloth. Stitch across both ends of the handle close to the edge. Reinforce first stitching twice on each end. (Fig. 6-3)

Step 4. Long Handle: Place the long handle four inches away from the long edge of the main piece of cloth. Stitch across each end of the long handle close to the edge of the main piece of cloth. After reinforcing the stitching three more times, sew a triangular reinforcing patch over both ends of handle.

Step 5. Install Zipper: Fold under both edges of the 37" side of the cloth ½" and stitch close to the folded edge. With the zipper foot on the sewing machine, sew one side of the zipper to the wrong side of the 37" side of the main piece. Be sure to center the zipper in the middle of the 37" side. With the zipper closed, place the zipper tape on the wrong side of the other 37" side and stitch with a zipper foot. You should now have a tube of cloth held together with a zipper. (Fig. 6-4) Sew both sides of the zipper with another row of stitching. Turn the tube right side out. Cut four 3" × 3" pieces of cloth from scraps of the material. Place two squares right sides together. Stitch three sides together and leave the fourth side open for turning the square right side

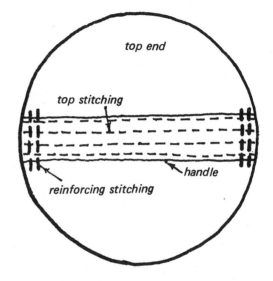

Fig. 6-3 *Top End Handle*

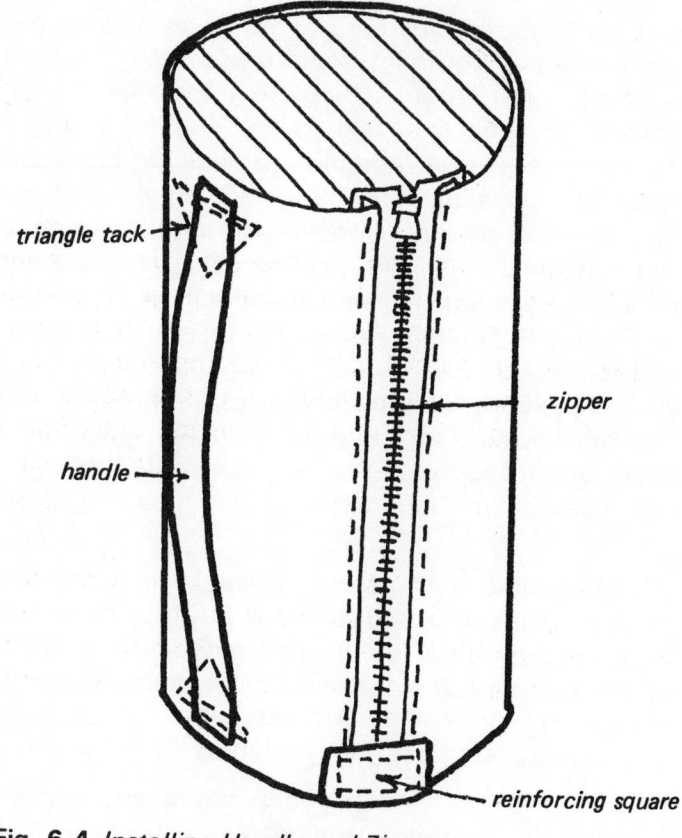

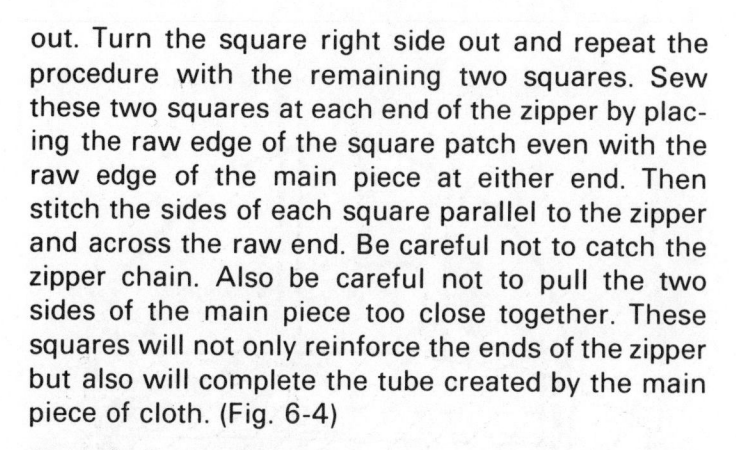

out. Turn the square right side out and repeat the procedure with the remaining two squares. Sew these two squares at each end of the zipper by placing the raw edge of the square patch even with the raw edge of the main piece at either end. Then stitch the sides of each square parallel to the zipper and across the raw end. Be careful not to catch the zipper chain. Also be careful not to pull the two sides of the main piece too close together. These squares will not only reinforce the ends of the zipper but also will complete the tube created by the main piece of cloth. (Fig. 6-4)

Step 6. Ends: Open the zipper and turn the duffel inside out. Pin ends of duffel into the tube, right

Fig. 6-4 *Installing Handle and Zipper*

sides together. Place the pins perpendicular to the seam line. Double stitch both ends into the tube. Zigzag the raw edge if possible. The raw ends of the handles will be inside the seam. Turn right side out. (Fig. 6-5)

Customizing

Design the inside or outside pocket before you begin to sew the duffel together. Remember to do all the sewing you can on each individual piece before assembling the duffel. Rope handles can be used instead of cloth handles if you prefer. Refer to Chapter 3 if you choose to use grommets to hold the line, or snaps to shut the pockets.

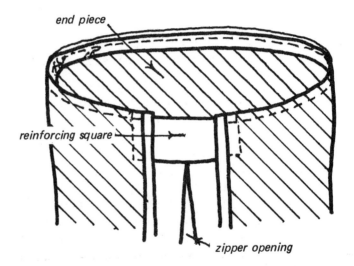

end piece

reinforcing square

zipper opening

Fig. 6-5 *Installing End Pieces*

Chapter seven

BUILDING AN AWNING OR SUN CANOPY

For the cruising boat or the little-used boat, an awning or sun canopy can save the boat from hours of finish-devouring sunlight, rain and snow. An awning can also increase the "living" space and create privacy.

A well-planned awning should incorporate pieces of cloth that will suit all your needs. For instance, part of the awning might be used as a cockpit canopy that can be easily put up, taken down and stowed. This canopy will protect the cockpit from too much sun and lower temperatures below decks. A winter-storage or long-layover cover can be attached to the cockpit canopy to form a full boat cover.

REQUIREMENTS OF AN AWNING

1. It should give maximum coverage while requiring minimum storage space.
2. It should be strong enough to remain standing in strong winds.
3. It should be of a color to deflect glare.
4. It should be easy to put up and take down.
5. It must be resistant to mildew and sun damage.
6. It should be pleasing to the eye and not detract from the lines of the vessel.
7. It should be water resistant, if not waterproof.

Photo 7-1 *Conestoga Awning*

Photo 7-2 *Aft Enclosure*

Photo 7-3 *Bimini Top*

Photo 7-4 *Dodger with Clear Vinyl Window*

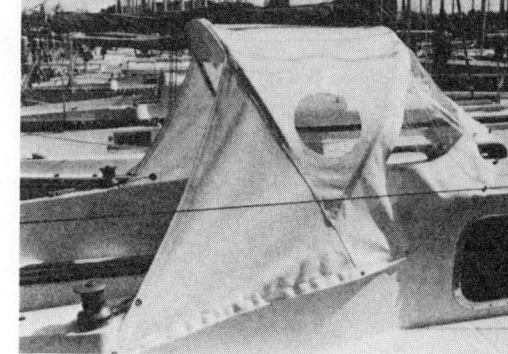

40

Suitable Materials

> Yachtcrylic
> Treated Canvas
> Weblon

Note: See Chapter 2 for descriptions of these materials and their uses.

BIMINI TOPS & COCKPIT DODGERS

There are too many variables involved for us to describe the construction of one highly specialized type of boat awning. These awnings, often called "Bimini Tops" on power yachts and "Cockpit Dodgers" on sailboats, are made of many mathematically figured, curved pieces of cloth. The curves differ as the angles of the stainless frames change. To build one of these tops from scratch would take more knowledge than we feel capable of imparting here, and the bent-tubing part of a Bimini top is outside the scope of this book. We can only encourage you to make the fabric part of a Bimini top or dodger by using your old one as a pattern.

Step 1. First make a careful inspection of the old top. Does it need changing? Possibly it has stretched out of shape. Take such alterations into account and mark them with a pen. Make lines right on the old top for the changes to be made in the new one.

Step 2. Carefully take the old top apart. Mark on the old cloth where batten pockets go, etc.

Step 3. Place the pieces of the old top on the new cloth and carefully mark around the edges of the pattern pieces. A felt pen should *not* be used on Weblon. Use a soft lead pencil. Be sure to allow for a full ½" seam allowance even though the pattern pieces may not have them. Label the new pieces to avoid confusion later on, but write only in the seam allowance.

Step 4. Cut the new pieces out and sew them together. Be sure to place batten pockets exactly where they were before. Check the new top against the old one as you go along.

Photo 7-5 *Paneled Awning with Bolt Rope, Battens and Side Curtains.*

Photo 7-6 *Paneled Awning without Battens. Held only by Bolt Rope, Halyard and Backstay.*

SAILBOAT OR MOTORSAILER AWNING

Necessary Materials

Number of yards of cloth required.
Fasteners: either grommets, snaps or twist locks
Line for rigging: #4, ⅛" nylon or Dacron
4 to 6 spools polyester thread
Battens (where necessary) These may be the collapsible aluminum type, wood or PVC pipe, or possibly your boat hook.

Measuring For Cloth

Step 1. First design the awning. Fig. 7-7 shows some basic awning layouts. Choose the layout that will best suit your needs. Most sailboat awnings are supported lengthwise by the mast and backstay or the mast and forestay. They are held *up* by halyards and booms, and held laterally by shrouds, the gallows frame and battens. The awnings are held *down* by lines to lifelines and deck fittings. A well-secured awning will not cause worry in high winds

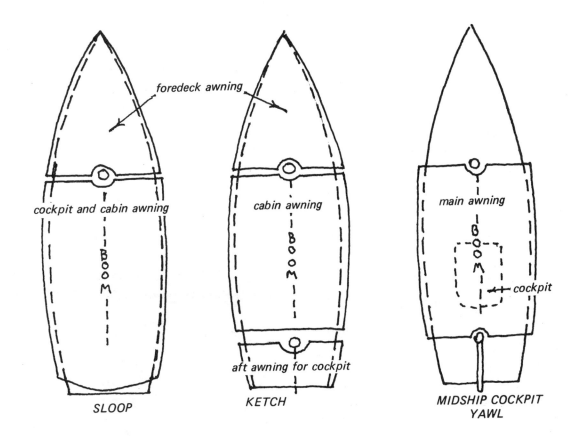

Fig. 7-7 Designing the Awning

43

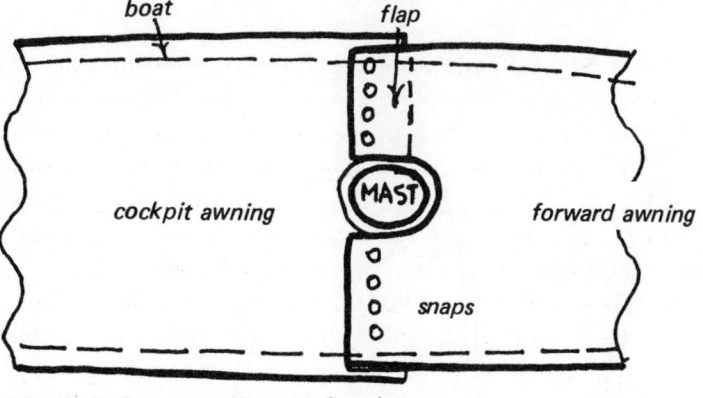

Fig. 7-8 *Snaps to Fasten Awning*

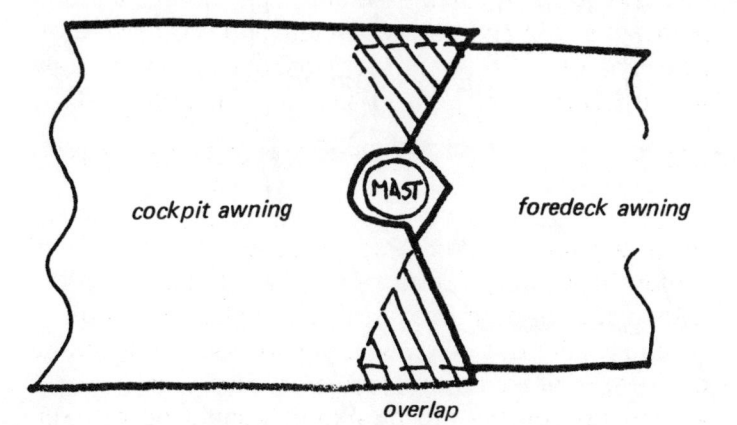

Fig. 7-9 *Overlap to Secure Awnings*

and will place little stress on any fitting to which it is fastened. Decide on the method you will use to fasten together the separate parts of the awning. Flaps that go from one section to another are suitable. (Fig. 7-8)

A better system than flaps is achieved if you design the sections of the awning so that they will overlap. (Fig. 7-9)

Each section is strung tightly to rigging, etc. The flaps should be made to take all normal strains.

Step 2. Measure the width of the parts of the boat you wish to cover. (Fig. 7-10)

Step 3. Measure the length of each fore-and-aft section you wish to cover. (Fig. 7-10)

Step 4. Place measurements on a diagram.

Step. 5. Take into consideration the width of the cloth you plan to use *(refer to Chapter 2)*, and figure how many panels of what length will be needed to cover each section of the boat. Add enough extra cloth for hems and reinforcing patches and figure the total yardage required. For large awnings or awnings with considerable curve in the edges, placing the panels athwartships may use less cloth than with fore-and-aft panels.

Step 6. Try to predetermine where battens will have to be placed to extend the awning out to the sides. Also figure as closely as possible where the mast or masts will fit in the canopy, whether slashes will be needed to accommodate backstays, topping lifts or shrouds, and where reinforcing patches will be needed for grommets not placed in hems.

MAKING THE AWNING

Step 1. Cut the lengths of cloth you will need for each piece. Make sure to allow 2″ extra for each hem. If batten pockets are to be used at the extreme ends of the awning, allow an extra 6″ or 8″ on each batten pocket end.

Step 2. Do whatever sewing you can on each panel before sewing the panels together. For instance, the canopy in our sketch has three panels. (Fig. 7-11) The two outer panels can be hemmed along the long sides before they are sewn to the middle panel. The mast cutout can be made, and the reinforcing patch for the supporting grommet can be sewn on the middle panel, before the three panels are sewn together. The less cloth you have to handle at one time the easier the job will be. Be particu-

45

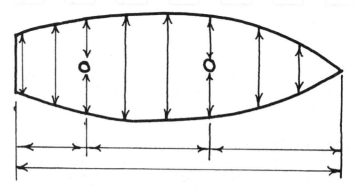

Fig. 7-10 *Measure Your Boat*

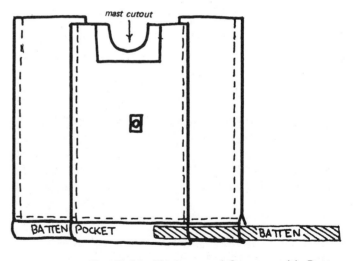

Fig. 7-11 *Three-panel Canopy with Batten*

larly careful about matching the right sides of each panel. Refer to Chapter 4 when making mast cutout, slashes and reinforcing patches.

Step 3. Sew all the panels together. Begin at an outside panel and work to the opposite outside panel. Make flat felled seams between panels as you go.

Step 4. Hem the remaining outside edges. In the example in Fig. 7-5 we need a batten pocket at the aft end. For this type of batten pocket:

    a. Fold over ¼" and stitch as in hemming.

    b. Fold over enough cloth to allow the batten to slip through easily and stitch the outer edge twice. (Fig. 7-11) This procedure is identical to making a hem except that the ends of the hem are not stitched down.

If you should need batten pockets anywhere in the middle of the awning:

    a. Cut a strip of cloth as long as the width of the

Photo 7-12 *PVC pipe provides curved support for awning.*

46

awning at the point where the batten pocket
must be sewn, and as wide as the diameter of
the batten plus 2".

b. Make a ¼" hem in both edges of the batten
pocket, and hem both ends.

c. Carefully pin the pocket in place, making sure
that you are placing the pocket at right angles
to the fore-and-aft centerline of the awning.

d. Stitch the pocket to the awning along both
long edges. Stitch these edges again for reinforcement.

You may wish to put a curve into the top of the
awning by using flexible PVC pipe as in Photos
7-12 and 7-13. In this case the batten pockets should
be sewn on in the same manner, but each batten
gets two pockets, one on either side of the centerline to allow you to slide the pipe through the bridle
that lifts the awning. This way, the weight of the
awning is carried by the poles rather than the grommets that the bridle goes through.

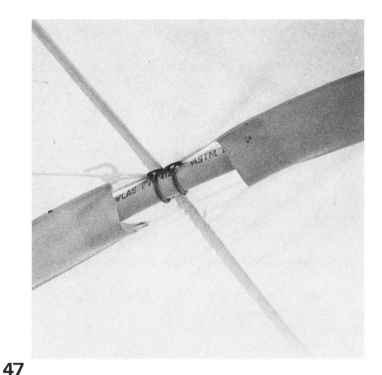

Photo 7-13 *Underside of Awning with PVC pipe,
     battens and bolt rope*

47

BOLT ROPE

For extra strength you may choose to sew a bolt rope down the center of the awning to hold up the awning between two masts, or the mast and backstay. This is highly recommended for large awnings. To do this:

a. Once all the panels have been sewn together and batten pockets have been sewn on, mark the center of the awning on the side that will face the deck of the boat. (You must have two batten pockets, one either side of the bolt rope —for each batten—as was discussed when using PVC pipe)

b. Fold the awning in half lengthwise on the centerline and place a piece of dacron rope that is 8' to 10' longer than the awning, inside the fold. With a zipper foot on the sewing machine stitch the two sides of the awning together around the rope. Stitch again for reinforcement.

c. Grommets should then be placed on *both* sides of the rope so that the bridle can go around the bolt rope. This allows the rope (rather than

the grommets) to carry the strain caused by the bridle. If battens are needed, place them in line with the bridle grommets and pass the batten through the bridle as well.

TIE-DOWNS AND OPTIONAL SIDE CURTAINS

Step 5. After the canopy is all sewn together, tie-downs must be made. This is usually done by spacing grommets around the canopy edges so they will line up with available stanchions, life lines, shrouds, and deck fittings that can be used to hold the canopy laterally or down. At the same time, install grommets for lacing around the mast, and in the reinforcing patches for the halyard bridle. You may also wish to place grommets in the ends of the batten pockets so you can tie the battens in and stretch the awning laterally. If a side curtain is desired to keep out early morning or afternoon sun, or to create privacy in the cockpit, you must first make the curtain of a size that will hang from the awning and shade the boat when the sun is low in the sky. Usually, one curtain is sufficient as it can be moved to follow the sun. This is achieved by setting snaps or grommets at equal distances all a-round the canopy, and having them line up with the snaps or grommets on the curtain no matter where you put it. Obviously, accurate equidistant spacing is required. Grommets will be required on the bottom of the side curtain to hold it down.

Tie 1/8" line to all tie-down and lacing grommets, and rig the bridle. When rigging your awning, be sure to pull the lines tight. A sloppy fit will cause more strain on it than the tension of the lines.

A well-designed and well-engineered awning will expand the livable space you have aboard, and protect your boat from sun, rain, snow and ice. If you've been careful and exact in your measuring and fitting, your completed awning should be one of which you can be very proud.

Chapter eight

SAIL COVERS

Since most sails today are made of Dacron or nylon it is important that they be protected whenever possible from the fiber-eating ultraviolet rays of the sun. Cotton sails also require a good cover of water-resistant material to keep out rain and thereby resist mildew and subsequent deterioration. A well-fitted sailcover will also add to the trim appearance of the vessel. This chapter will discuss how to make a simple sail cover that can be modified to fit any boat's boom. As you design your own sailcover, take into account any fittings, lines, winches or special requirements that your particular cover should have to do the job attractively and adequately.

MATERIALS

There are a number of materials one can choose for sail covers. 8- or 10-oz. canvas is adequate when you treat it with waterproofing. However, since the waterproofing will not last long and since untreated canvas is susceptible to mildew, we suggest a synthetic such as acrylic or a factory-treated canvas such as Vivatex. The treatment given to Vivatex is far superior to a "home" treatment of plain canvas. Plastic- or rubber-coated materials are not suitable for sail covers. It is important that the cover "breathe" so that the sail will not mildew. Coated materials are also poor choices because they eventually lose their coating from the repeated rolling or wadding up a sailcover undergoes when not stretched on the boom. You may choose nylon material as it is a lightweight cloth and will stow in a small space when not in use. However, nylon will crinkle noisily in the wind and may stretch after it has been pulled tight for awhile. It also allows considerable sunlight to reach the sails if it is lightweight, and will not last as long as Vivatex or acrylic.

FASTENINGS

Of all the fastenings discussed in Chapter 3, we suggest using a grommet and sail hook combination to fasten most sail covers. This system is simple and easy to install and will not fail from repeated use or water corrosion. It consists of placing a pair of grommets on one side of the cover to oppose each sail hook. Shock cord is then knotted through the grommets and hooked over the sail hook.

If you have a zigzag sewing machine with an adjustable feeder, you can sew the hooks on easily by putting the feeder in its down position, as if sewing on a button, and setting the zigzag scale to just miss the metal. Otherwise, the hooks can be sewn on by hand. We don't recommend that you use one continuous length of shock cord, threaded through all the grommets the length of the sailcover, for two reasons. The first involves cost. Shock cord is expensive, and if the shock cord breaks in one place, the entire length will need replacing rather than, say, a 6" piece. The second reason involves safety. If this 12' or 16' of shock cord should snap loose in a storm and snag on gear or people, it could cause an injury.

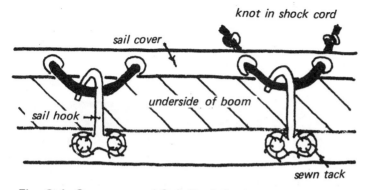

knot in shock cord

sail cover

underside of boom

sail hook →

sewn tack

Fig. 8-1 *Grommet and Sail Hook System*

Lightweight line can be used to tie the sail cover snugly around the top of the sail and mast to make fastening the shock cord easier. Such line can also be used to tie the after end of the cover around the boom. If cutouts are necessary for lines, etc., light line can also be threaded through grommets to lace the cutout together after the cover is in place.

You will see some beautiful sail covers that are fastened at the front of the mast with a zipper. This is very attractive and impressive, but we don't feel that the amateur should attempt this type of closure on a sail cover. The fit of the cover must be exactly

right or the zipper will be nearly impossible to close, or in the case of an oversize cover, will bump and hang terribly. The grommet and sail hook system allows you to "take up the slack" in the cover in case it doesn't fit exactly the way you had planned.

MAKING A PATTERN

If you have old sailcovers that fit to your satisfaction you will have no problem using them as patterns for your new covers. Simply rip the old cover apart carefully, add seam allowances and cut the new pieces around the old ones. Be careful to note "right side" and "wrong side" in pieces that are not reversible. If you don't have a cover to use as a pat-

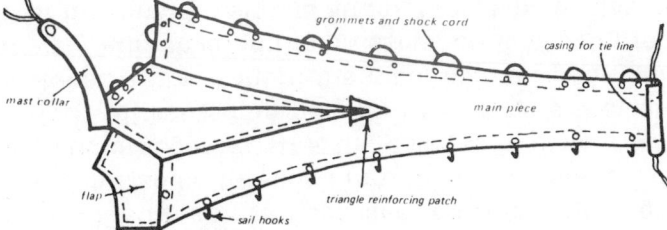
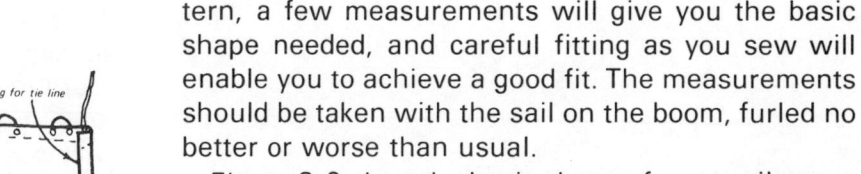

grommets and shock cord

casing for tie line

mast collar

main piece

flap

triangle reinforcing patch

sail hooks

Fig. 8-2 *Basic Shape of Sail Cover*

Photo 8-3 *Sail Cover Customized for Climbing Brackets*

tern, a few measurements will give you the basic shape needed, and careful fitting as you sew will enable you to achieve a good fit. The measurements should be taken with the sail on the boom, furled no better or worse than usual.

Figure 8-2 gives the basic shape of most sailcovers for sails on booms connected to masts. Covers for sails on booms connected to stays or for gaff-headed sails will have a flatter and smaller inset but will be basically the same shape. This figure is also optimum in that there is not a seam down the middle of the cover. This portion of any sailcover receives the most direct sunlight, and the most wear. If your sail cover must be considerably wider than the width of the cloth you are using, you will have to put a seam down the middle of the cover. If it needs to be only slightly wider, however, it is advisable to make the cover as it is described here and add the extra width to the bottom edges of the cover.

One more clue before measuring: The sail cover should have at least a two-inch gap at the underside of the boom to allow the shock cord to stretch and create tension on the cover. Be sure that you remember this when adding hem allowances.

Figure 8-4 gives all the measurements needed for most basic sail covers. After you have these measurements, you can measure for cutouts or winch covers or adaptations for your particular rig. It is usually not advisable, though, to cut any holes or slashes until most of the basic cover is put together. Measuring for these custom changes on the sail cover itself, in place on the boom, insures a more exact fit.

CUTTING AND CONSTRUCTION

Main Piece
Step 1. Take measurements A, L, H, G, F, & E shown in Fig. 8-4. These measurements will give you the shape of the main piece of the cover. Allow for a 2" hem and a 2" gap under the boom. Allowing for a 1" hem but actually sewing a 2" hem will provide the space required under the boom.

Step 2. Mark these measurements on the cloth, being sure to center the measurements on the material. At this point you can tell if you will need to add cloth to the bottom edges of the cover, or if you will have to cut two main pieces and sew them

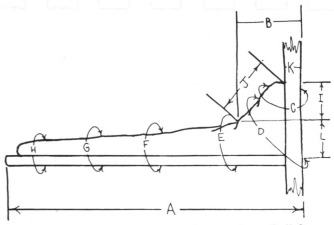

Fig. 8-4 *Measurements for a Sail Cover*

Photo 8-5 *Staysail Sail Cover with Flat Inset*

55

together. H, G, F, and E measurements are circumferences. Use them as flat measurements when making the main piece in one piece, divide them in half when cutting the main piece in two pieces.

Step 3. Cut and sew the main piece. Being careful to add hem and seam allowances where you need them, and remembering the fore and aft ends as well, cut the main piece out and hem the side or bottom edges. Fold over the aft end of the main piece to make a casing for the drawstring that will tie around the end of the boom, and stitch. Light line can be threaded through this casing by stabbing a large safety pin into the line and using it to thread the line through.

Mast Inset
Step 4. Measurements J and B will help you determine how far to cut the main piece for the mast inset, but do not cut this until the mast inset has been cut. Use measurements J, B, I and K to get the angles for the mast inset. First take measurement B and mark it on a straight edge of cloth. Then take measurement I and mark it on your cloth using one end of your B measurement as the bottom starting point. Then place the K measurement, which is the

diameter of the mast, parallel to the B measurement using the top of the I measurement as a starting place. The J measurement should be the same as the

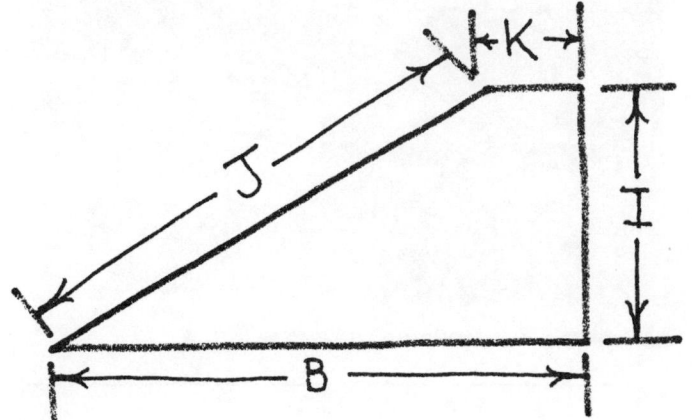

Fig. 8-6 *Mast Inset*

distance between the open ends of K and B. If it is not, juggle the I measurement until it fits or make J a curved line to accommodate the sail. Allow 2″ for hemming the I edge, 1" for hemming the K edge and ½" seam allowances on the J and B edges.

Step 5. Cut two of the pieces described in Step 4 to make the right and left sides of the mast inset, and sew the J edges together with a flat felled seam.

Step 6. Transfer the length of the B edge from the mast inset to the main piece of the cover. Slash the main piece down the center exactly to the B measurement.

Step 7. Place the right sides of the main piece and the mast inset together, lining up the middle of each piece. Stitch the B seam on the left side, lift the presser foot and rotate the pieces so you can stitch the right side. Pinning these parts together will undoubtedly make it more accurate. Flat-fell this seam if there is enough cloth to turn under. If not, zigzag the seam allowance to the cover. Sew a re-inforcement patch over the point at which the apex of the inset meets the main piece. This will strengthen this area and camouflage any trouble you had in making this corner. Hem the right and left forward, or I and L, edges of the sail cover. Make a 1" hem at the K edge.

Flap

Step 8. The flap is used to cover the front of the mast and any winches that may be mounted there. It should be as tall as the sail cover and as wide as needed to do the job. Hem the flap on all edges with a ½" seam. Sew the right side of the flap to the wrong side of the starboard side of the sailcover.

Mast Collar

Step 9. The mast collar is used to secure the forward end of the cover around the mast and external halyards to make fastening the shock cord easier. This piece of cloth should be approximately 2" wide and long enough to go around the mast at least one and a half times. Hem this piece all the way around and sew it to the top of the mast inset at K. It is usually most effective if the collar is sewn to the outside edge of the mast inset. A grommet should be placed in the very end of the tail and a line fastened to it that will go around the mast.

FINISHING

Step 10. Place grommets on the port side of the bottom and forward edges, and the hooks opposite them on the starboard side of the cover. Place these pairs about 15" to 18" apart. The hooks should be tacked in each loop. Put the cover in place and thread shock cord through the grommets, adjusting the length of the cord so that the cover fits snugly. An overhand or figure-8 knot works very well for securing the shock cord. If you have mast-mounted winches and wish to make built-in covers for them in the sail cover, refer to Chapter 10 and modify the design to fit into your sail cover. Usually these covers wear out quickly and it is just as attractive to allow enough length in the main piece of your sail cover simply to go around the winches as it circles sail and mast. A sacrificial piece of cloth may be sewn to the inside of the sail cover where winches may rub, to save wear on the cover itself.

Chapter nine

A SIMPLE WIND CHUTE

A wind chute is a device that funnels breezes below decks to cool the interior and ventilate stuffy places. It is a necessity and a blessing when cruising the tropics, and a welcome one in most warm climates where little breeze flows in the evening. In poorly ventilated boats that lack opening ports or Dorade ventilators, a wind chute will do an amazing job to help keep the boat's interior fresh and dry.

This particular wind chute has four wind catchers that will catch air from any direction and divert it below. Whether sitting at dockside or lying at anchor into the wind or current this wind chute will funnel air below without having to be repositioned as the wind changes direction. The chute is placed in a forward hatch and is secured by two wood dowels that are placed in the chute from below deck. A jib or genoa halyard is then used to lift the chute and hold it taut, and this lift causes the dowels to pull up tightly against the underside of the hatch frame. The chute described here is designed to fit any forward hatch up to 30" square. You can, however, customize the chute so that the bottom of it fits tightly around the outside of your forward hatch frame and fastens with snaps rather than dowels. This can be done by making the bottom measurements of the wind tunnel the same as the size of your hatch. For instance, the wind tunnel here is 30" square. If your forward hatch frame is 24 × 30, cut two of the side panels of the wind tunnel 25 inches wide at the bottom and cut the other two panels 31 inches wide. Allowing for half inch seams this will give you finished dimensions of 24 × 30. If you choose to customize your windchute, the screen will have to be sewn higher in the wind tunnel to accommodate the hatch frame. Customizing is nice but not necessary, as this wind chute works very well in all hatches up to 30" square.

Dimensions: Top 29" × 29" (approx.);
Bottom 29" × 29" (approx.);
Height 6'.

Photo 9-1 *Wind Chute*

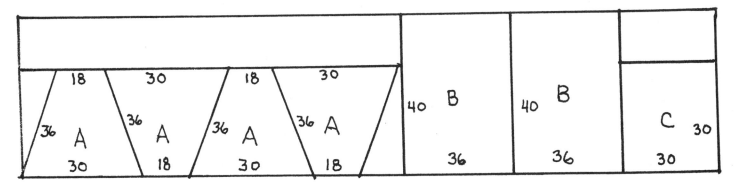

Fig. 9-2 *Layout for Cutting Wind Chute*

MATERIALS

  6 yds. nylon spinnaker cloth, preferably 1.5 oz.
  248" of nylon webbing, 1 to 2 inches wide
  9 grommets
  12" of light line
  4 ½" wood dowels, 42" long
  2 spools polyester thread
  1 pc. fiberglass screen 31" square

CONSTRUCTION

Step 1. Cut the following pieces:
  4 panels for wind tunnel (A) 30" x 36" x 18"
  2 panels for wind catcher (B) 40" × 36"
  1 top (C) 30" x 30"
  1 screen (D) 31" × 31"

Wind Tunnel

Step 2. Place two of the "A" pieces right sides together so that the edges match. Stitch along one long edge ½" from the edge of the cloth. Open the two pieces so that they lie flat. Sew a flat-felled seam by folding the seam allowance under. Repeat this procedure with the remaining two "A" pieces, then sew the third and fourth seams to complete the tunnel.

Step 3. Fold ¼" of the bottom edge of the wind tunnel to the outside. Stitch. Stitch the nylon webbing around the bottom of the wind tunnel so that it covers the raw edge of the folded edge yet extends a bit below the bottom of the spinnaker cloth. Overlap the beginning and end of the tape and stitch securely.

Step 4. Hem the top edge of the wind tunnel by folding the material over twice. This hem should be as narrow as possible.

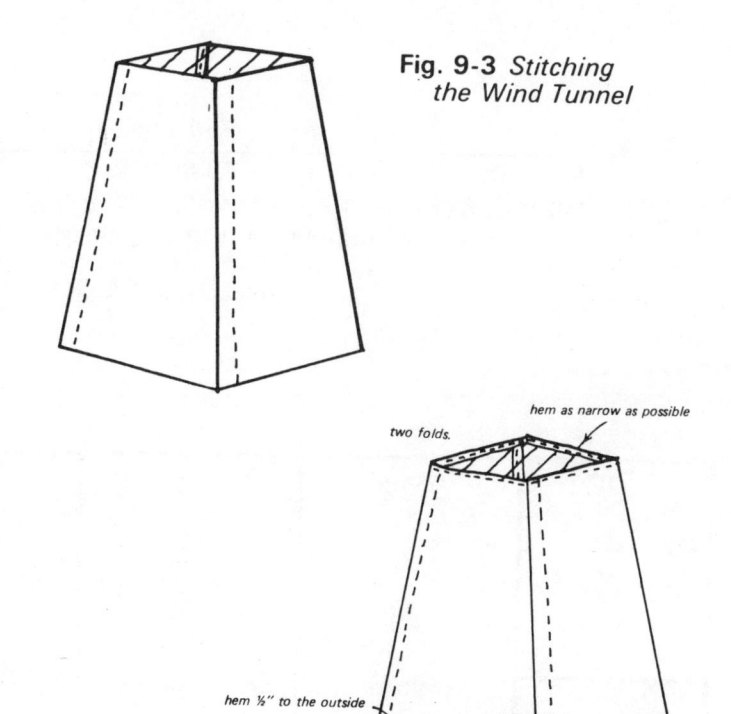

Fig. 9-3 *Stitching the Wind Tunnel*

two folds.

hem as narrow as possible

hem ½" to the outside

overlap

nylon webbing

Fig. 9-4 *Placing Webbing and Hem in Wind Tunnel*

62

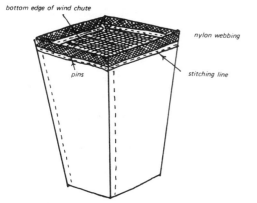

bottom edge of wind chute

nylon webbing

pins

stitching line

Fig. 9-5 *Pinning the Screen*

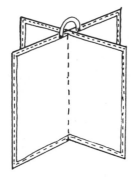

Fig. 9-6 *Wind Catcher*

Step 5. Screen (optional). Pin the screen to the top edge of the nylon webbing and inside the bottom of the wind tunnel. Place pins perpendicular to the stitching line. Make double folds in the corners of the screen to take up the ease. Stitch all the way around the screen.

Wind Catcher

Step 6. Hem all four outside edges of both B pieces by folding over ¼″ once and ¼″ again, and then stitching all around. Place one B piece over the other, matching all edges. With the longest edges as top and bottom, find the center line by folding the two pieces in half, matching the 36″ edges. Pin the center line and stitch the two pieces together along this line. Sew a small loop of nylon webbing to the top of the wind catcher over the center seam to use as a lifting ring.

Sew Wind Catcher to Wind Tunnel

Step 7. We want the wind catcher to fit inside the wind tunnel as if it were an "X". To do this we will sew the bottom corners along the vertical edges of the wind catcher to the corner seams of the wind tunnel so that 6" of the wind catcher is inside the tunnel.

Now you will find that the diagonal of the wind catcher (36") is *longer* than the diagonal of the top of the wind tunnel (25½") thus creating a "bagginess" in the catcher. This extra material balloons inward as the wind is caught, directing a maximum flow of air below decks.

Take the 36" side of one of the flaps of the wind catcher and place the bottom 6" of it inside the wind tunnel and pin it to one of the tunnel's seams. Working around the tunnel pin the 36" side of the next flap to the next corner and then the next flap to the next corner and then the final flap to the last corner of the wind tunnel. Stitch each flap of the catcher in place.

Top

Step 8. Hem all edges of the top piece C as you did the wind catcher pieces. Sew the nylon webbing to the outside edge of the top so that it makes a curtain

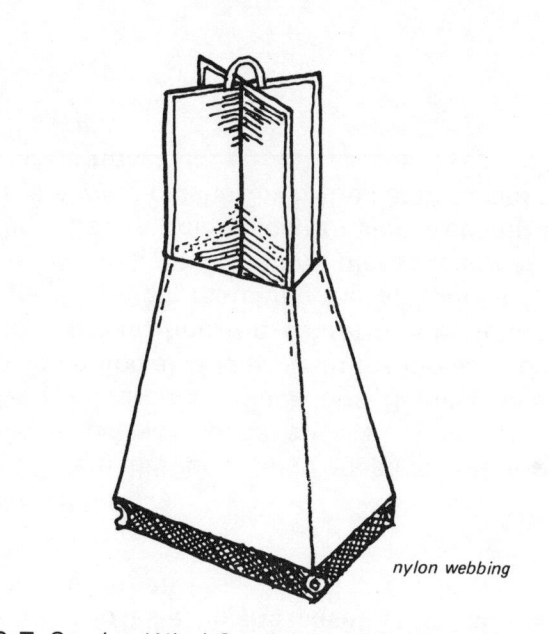

nylon webbing

Fig. 9-7 *Sewing Wind Catcher to Wind Tunnel*

that hangs down below the top ¾ of an inch. The grommets that hold the dowels in place will be set in this webbing so there must be enough room for them. To do this begin sewing the webbing on to the

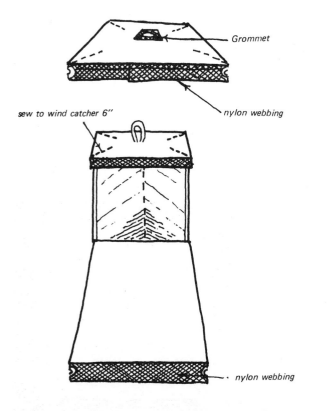

sew to wind catcher 6"

Grommet

nylon webbing

nylon webbing

Fig. 9-8 *Sewing Top to Wind Catcher*

top in the middle of one edge. When you get to the corner, put the needle of the machine down through the webbing and cloth exactly at the corner. Then turn the top 90 degrees and bend the webbing around so that it matches the edge of the top again. Stitch the webbing flat to the next corner and repeat the corner procedure. Continue in this manner until the webbing has been sewn all around the top. Overlap the ends of the webbing and stitch securely. Turn the corners right-side-out so that the tape extends down from the top like a short curtain all the way around. Find the middle of the top and sew a small patch of nylon webbing to the very center on the wrong side of the top. This patch will reinforce the grommet that will eventually be placed there.

Step 9. Now you will find that the diagonal of the wind catcher (40") is *shorter* than the diagonal of the top (42½"). The fact that the sewn flaps do not extend all the way to the corners of the top leaves room for the installation of the dowels. (Step 10) Secure the top to the wind catcher by sewing 6" of the top edge of each wind-catcher flap to the top piece, placing each flap as close to the corners as possible.

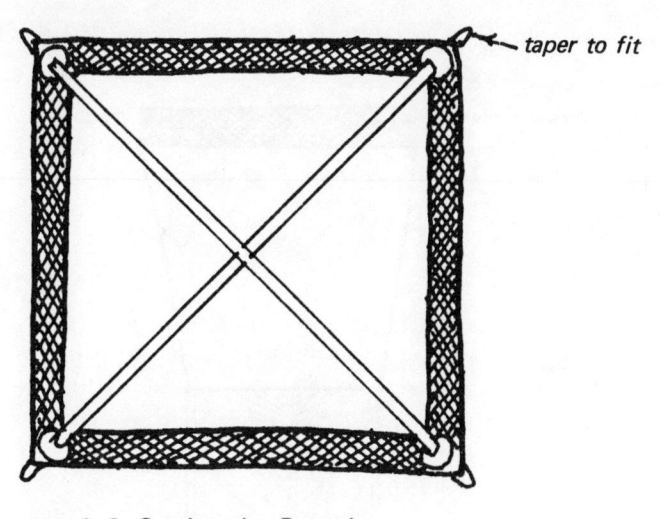

taper to fit

Fig. 9-9 *Setting the Dowels*

Finishing

Step 10. Set grommets in all four corners of the top and bottom nylon webbing. Set one grommet in the center patch of the top. Tie the small piece of line to the nylon loop at the top of the wind catcher. Thread the other end of this line through the grommet in the middle of the top. Place two dowels corner to corner in the bottom and the top of the wind chute. Center them and mark them so that they will extend slightly beyond the edges of the wind chute. Cut the dowels to size and taper the ends to points so that they will fit tightly into corner grommets.

Rig the chute aboard and enjoy wonderful fresh air below.

Chapter ten

CUSTOM COVERS FOR ON-DECK EQUIPMENT

Because of the damaging effects of the elements to almost anything on a boat it is often desirable to cover items such as brightwork, brass and machinery as much as is possible whenever they are not in use. A binnacle is a prime example, as are winches, windlasses, deck boxes, air conditioners, hatch covers, depth sounders and steering wheels. Each cover for these things is usually customized, but with a few instructions you will be able to design and construct a cover that will fit each item. Note for example the resemblance between a ditty bag and many other covers. The methods of design, measurement and construction you have learned from other projects in this book will help in making a customized cover.

MATERIAL

The cloth to use is canvas, preferably treated, or acrylic. When you cover something to protect it from sun, wind and water don't create another problem by covering it with a material that doesn't "breathe." Moisture will eventually get under any cover and it must be allowed to get back out. Choose fastenings that will achieve closure *simply*. Often a drawstring around the bottom is the best (and easiest) method of fastening a cover.

67

Photo 10-1 *Square Hatch Cover*

Photo 10-2 *Custom Hatch Cover*

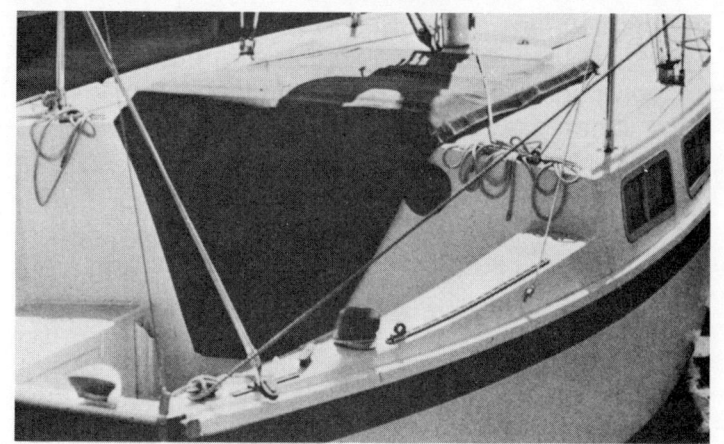

Photo 10-3 *Binnacle and Wheel Cover Fastened with Snaps*

Photo 10-4 *Binnacle and Wheel Cover Fastened with Velcro*

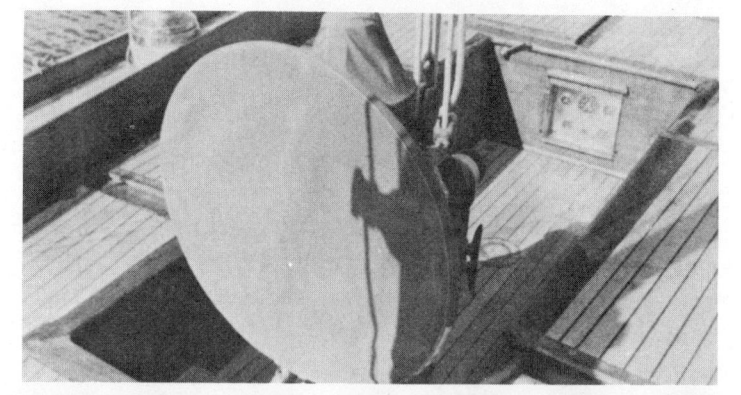
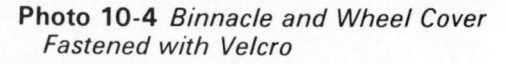

DESIGNING A PATTERN

Step 1. Look at the object and analyze the angles and surface areas to be covered. For instance, a winch has a top, sides that are continuous, and a 90° angle between the two. A hatch cover may have a top, and three or four sides—three of which could be different shapes—and the angle between a side and the top may be greater than 90°. The top of a hatch may be curved, and the two pairs of sides may be different heights. An air conditioner will probably have a top, three sides and an exposed bottom and back. The angles will probably be 90 degrees. Draw a sketch of the object that you want to cover and label each surface area to be covered.

Step 2. Decide which sides you can make with one continuous piece of cloth, and which sides must be cut exactly to shape. For instance, a winch cover needs to have one circular piece of cloth for the top and one continuous length of cloth for the sides that will go all the way around, much like a ditty bag. A hatch cover can probably be made with one piece for the top and one strip for the sides. However, de-

pending on the type of hatch, it may be more desirable to have separate pieces for each side that are eventually sewn together to make one strip.

Step 3. Take accurate measurements for the pieces you have decided to use. Remember to allow ½″ for seams and 2″ for hems. Place these measurements on your drawing.

Step 4. Figure the amount of cloth required to complete the job. Refer to Chapter 2 for the widths of cloth that are available.

Step 5. Decide how you will fasten the cover: snaps, grommets, Velcro, drawstring.

Step 6. Measure and draw the pieces on the cloth. If the cover you are making has many angles or curves that are important to fit, making a paper pattern first may simplify the job considerably.

Step 7. Stitch the pieces together, remembering to do all the sewing you can on the small pieces, and planning ahead so that you do not forget anything.

Step 8. Attach the fastenings and fit.

SPECIFIC EXAMPLE

Winch Covers

A beautiful winch cover can be made with a yard of treated or acrylic canvas, some ½" elastic and thread. All it really involves is making a ditty bag within a ditty bag and placing it upside down on the winch.

Step 1. Top: Cut one circle of cloth the exact circumference of the top of the winch plus ½" seam allowance. (Refer to Chapter 5 on how to draw a circle).

Step 2. Outside Piece: Cut one piece of cloth the length of the circumference of the circle, and the height of the winch, plus ½"for seam allowance and 1½" for hem. This will be the outside layer of cloth.

Step 3. Inside Piece: Cut one piece of cloth the same length as the outside piece but make it the height of the winch from the top to its narrowest circumference, plus 1" for the casing, and ½" for seam allowance. This piece will be inside the outside cover and will grip the winch with elastic.

Step 4. Stitch the side seam of the inside piece. Make a ¾" casing at the bottom edge. Stitch close to the edge. When stitching, leave an opening ½" wide to thread the elastic through.

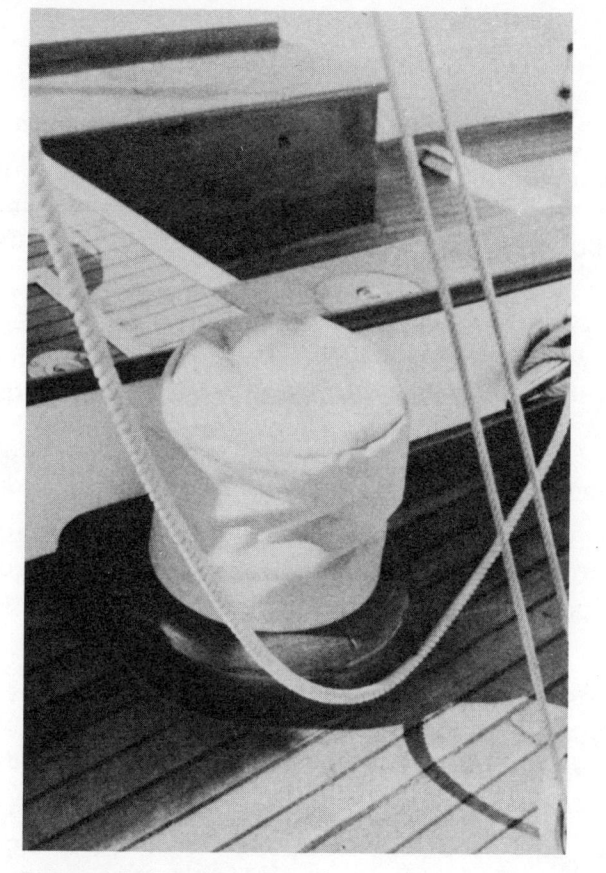

Photo 10-5 *Winch Cover*

70

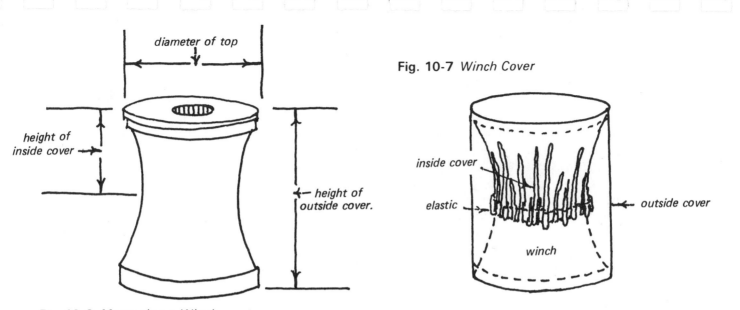

Fig. 10-6 *Measuring a Winch*

Fig. 10-7 *Winch Cover*

Step 5. Cut a piece of elastic that will fit snugly around the smallest part of the winch and add ½" for sewing. Put a safety pin through one end of the elastic and thread it through the casing. Holding both ends of the elastic overlap them and stitch them together. Allow the elastic to slip into the casing and stitch closed the opening in the casing.

Step 6. Stitch the side seam of the outside piece. Hem this piece so that it will just cover the winch plus ½" for the top seam allowance.

Step 7. Place the outside piece inside the inside piece so that the wrong sides of both pieces are facing you.

Step 8. Pin the top piece to both side pieces, right sides together. Stitch twice around. Turn right side out and cover your winch.

71

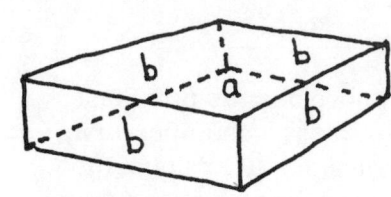
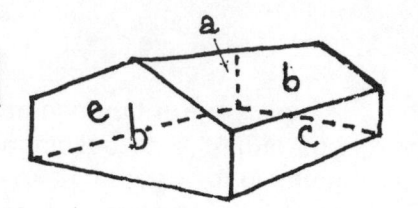

Fig. 10-8 *Hatch Cover*

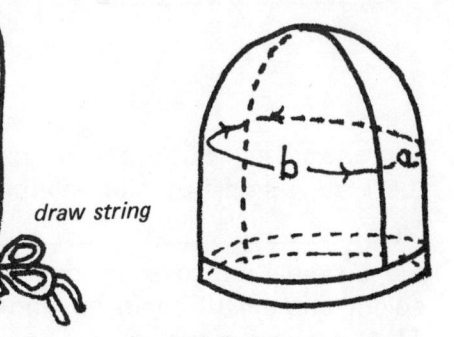
draw string

IDEAS FOR DESIGNING SPECIAL EQUIPMENT COVERS

Fig. 10-9 *Binnacle Cover*

Two plans for laying out and making canvas hatch covers are shown in Fig. 10-8. The one on the left is the simplest form of hatch cover, all square corners and right angles. It can be made from two pieces of fabric—one for the top (*a*) and one continuous piece (*b*) for the four sides. The version on the right is more complex due to its shape, and requires five separate pieces of fabric—two ends (*b*), two long sides *(c)*, and one top (*a*), which folds to form the two facets of the pitched top. Both these hatch covers are measured and assembled by the methods already described in earlier chapters.

In the next sketch, Fig. 10-9, we see two versions of a binnacle cover. Each is made with two pieces of fabric. The one on the left is the simpler version, having one piece for a continuous side, and a second piece for a top. Its assembly, with a drawstring

to hold it tight to the binnacle base, closely follows that of the ditty bag described earlier. The one on the right, also made of two pieces, is somewhat more demanding, but results in a more professional-looking job. The two pieces in this version are cut to match the angle of the binnacle at the top and are then sewn together to achieve a close fit.

In Fig. 10-10 the sketch shows a Depth Sounder Cover. It is a fairly straightforward job of sewing a "box." Like a cigar box, the front swings open to permit the depth sounder to be read without removing the entire cover, and this opening flap is held in the closed position with Velcro "latches." One method of holding this (bottomless) cover in place is shown: Two elastic straps are sewn to the bottom of one end; when putting on the cover, you slip these straps under the depth sounder and fasten these straps with

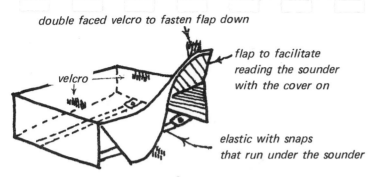

double faced velcro to fasten flap down

flap to facilitate
reading the sounder
with the cover on

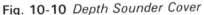
velcro

elastic with snaps
that run under the sounder

Fig. 10-10 *Depth Sounder Cover*

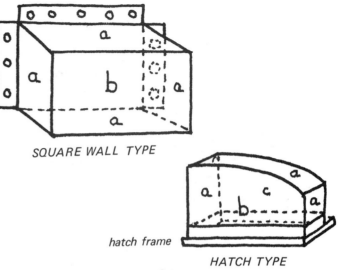

snap tape to snap
to bulkheads

SQUARE WALL TYPE

hatch frame

HATCH TYPE

Fig. 10-11 *Air Conditioner Cover*

snaps or Velcro strips at the bottom of the opposite side.

The fourth idea (Fig. 10-11) shows a custom-made cover for an air conditioner—or rather, two versions of such a cover. The first is a simple rectangular "box" for a bulkhead-mounted air conditioner—commonly seen on power yachts—and the second is for a hatch-cover or cabin-top installation, more frequently seen on auxiliary sailboats. The power yacht version is made with just two pieces of fabric, Piece *a*, which provides three sides *and* the flaps which hold the snaps that attaches the cover to the cabin top, and Piece *b*, the top of the cover. As always, careful measurement should precede the routine assembly job. On the right in the sketch, the sailboat version requires three pieces of fabric: Piece *a* making two ends and the top, and Pieces *b* and *c* for the two sides. This assembly method can be adapted to a number of varied shapes, as dictated by the unit to be covered and the installation site. Either snaps, Velcro or turn buttons will serve as closures and hold-downs for the cover.

Studying these plans will allow you to see how you might lay out other custom covers. It is best to keep to a minimum the number of pieces required for any project.

73

Photo 10-12 *Air Conditioner Cover Fastened with Shock Cord*

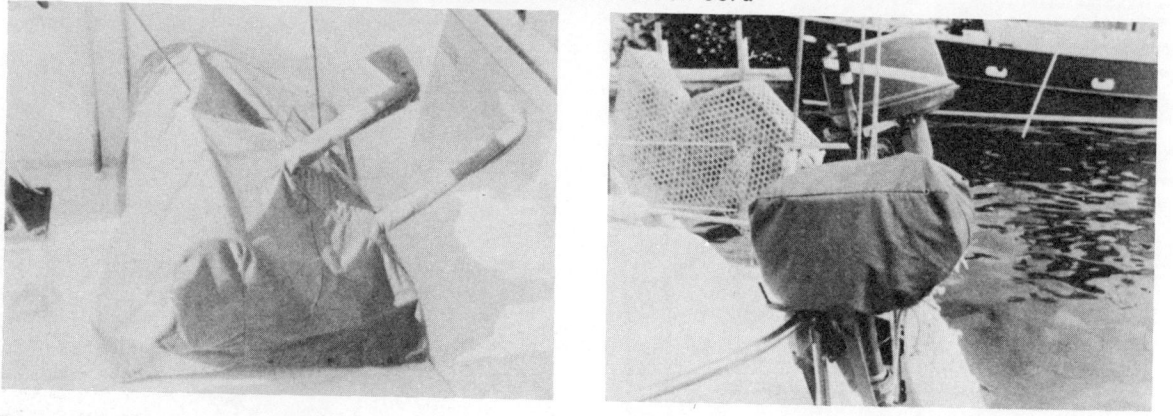

Photo 10-13 *Windlass Cover*

Photo 10-14 *Outboard Cover*

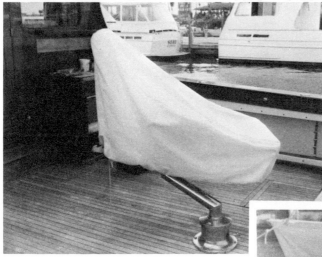

Photo 10-15 *Fishing Chair Cover*

Photo 10-16 *Combination Wind Scoop-Rain Shield held by Halyard and Velcro Tape*

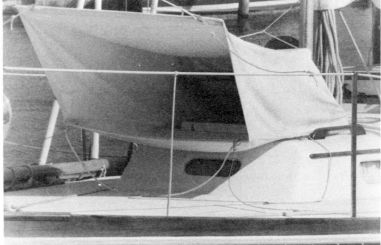

75

Chapter eleven

SECURE YOUR SHIP
WITH WEATHER CLOTHS

Weather cloths, or splash curtains, are designed to make the cockpit or bridge area of a boat more comfortable and less vulnerable to spray. They also add to the psychological security of the crew and increase the privacy of the cockpit. Weather cloths are usually laced to the life lines with light line through grommets or, in the case of some power yachts, snapped or screwed on to permanent structures and railings. Weather cloths not only add comfort and security to a vessel, but also can add to the beauty of the boat.

MATERIALS
Weblon can be used for weather cloths because they are free standing and don't seal off wood or metal. Weblon also cleans easily. Power yachts traditionally use Weblon, but auxiliary yachts often shy away from the shiny plastic and choose acrylic or treated canvas. All three of these fabrics are excellent for weather cloths.

If you plan to lace the curtains between lifelines and rail cap, you will need enough grommets to put one every 6" to 8" along the top and sides of the

Photo 11-1 *Weather Cloths for a Power Yacht*

If you plan to fasten the weather cloths to permanent wooden or metal structures, choose the proper Lift-a-Dot snap tops and wood or metal screw-type snap bottoms. Be prepared to replace these fastenings occasionally.

MEASURING

An effective weather cloth on a sailing vessel should run from about midships all the way aft. If you have a gate aft of midships in your lifeline or railing, a separate weather cloth should be made for the gate area. Otherwise, a weather cloth should be one continuous piece of cloth. Sailboats rarely need a weather cloth across the stern, but the design of your stern pulpit may make it advisable to continue the cloth right around to the other side. Power yachts usually enclose the bridge area entirely with the weather cloths ending and restarting at appropriate corners or gates.

When lacing the weather cloths between lifelines and stanchions, it is advisable to sew the cloths slightly smaller than the space to be filled so that the cloth can be stretched tightly. When fastening the cloths with snaps it is most important that the cloths be sewn exactly to size.

curtains. You will also need some tie-downs along the bottom, but be careful to place them only where you have something to tie to. One continuous length of light line will be necessary to tie the sides and top of the curtain. Small pieces can be used to tie the bottom edge. Have enough thread to do the whole job. Three large spools of polyester thread should be enough to sew two 8' x 30" curtains.

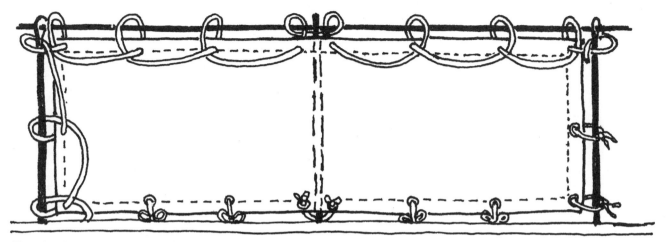

Fig. 11-2 *Lacing the Weather Cloth*

Step 1. Measure the length at *both* top and bottom.

Step 2. Measure the width at several intervals and at both ends. Note these measurements on a sketch diagram.

Step 3. Make note of any slashes or cutouts that are necessary for gear attached to stanchions or winch leads or mooring chocks. The weather cloth should be rigged outboard of your stanchions, but inboard of life rings, if you carry them.

Step 4. Add extra cloth for a 2" hem all the way around the outside

CONSTRUCTION

Step 1. Cut out the weather cloths.

Step 2. Hem all edges. Stitch once on the outside and once on the inside edge of the hem.

Step 3. Make any necessary slashes or cutouts. You may want to remeasure at this point, by holding

79

the weather cloth in place to make sure the cutouts are located accurately.

Step 4. Measure and mark for grommets, snaps or screws by placing four grommets in the corners of the cloth and rigging them tightly in place. With a marking pen, mark where the additional grommets should go. On the top lacing, the grommets should be 6" to 8" apart. On the bottom and sides, place grommets where they will reach something you can tie to on the rail or deck. For instance, pad eyes, stanchions, or cheek blocks make excellent tie-downs for weather cloths. Or, you can install special eyes to use as tie-downs. *The heavy stress is on the top and ends of the cloths,* so not as many tie-downs are needed on the bottom.

Step 5. Install the grommets or snaps in the cloths.

Step 6. Rig the weather cloths. If you are using the grommet system: with light line of continuous length, lace the top with half hitches all along the life line. Then attach sides and bottom with appropriate lengths of line.

If you are using snaps, fastened to a railing or deck, install the snaps in the appropriate place beginning at one end, then work along the top and bottom equally, stretching the cloth tightly as you go until you reach the other end. Install the final end snaps.

To cover the windows of a power yacht, follow the instructions for making weather cloths. Be sure to make the cover wide enough to be fastened securely to the frame of the window with snaps.

Photo 11-3 *Weather Cloths for Windows*

Photo 11-4 *Name Appliqued to Weather Cloth*

Chapter twelve

RIGGING A RAIN CATCHER

When cruising to places where drinking water is expensive, brackish or nonexistent, it's really practical to have a simple means of collecting rain water which, incidentally, is delicious to drink and great for bathing. The heavily chlorinated water which most of us drink is awful compared with pure rain water.

If you have a Bimini top or dodger that is normally kept rigged, it's a simple matter to install rain-draining funnels in the top of it. (Refer to the following instructions on installing the funnel.) Before doing so, however, locate the lowest point on the Bimini top or dodger and place one or two funnels there. Experiment with slacking off the tension on the top's supports to create better drainage.

It is important that the rain catcher be capable of being rigged in strong winds, so it's not advisable to rig a rain-catching funnel in a large awning that could be damaged in bad weather. If, however, you have a small cockpit awning that is likely to be rigged when it rains or storms, placing a rain-catching funnel in it will relieve you of carrying a separate rain catcher.

The following instructions are for a 6' x 8' rectangular rain catcher, a size we find practical. It consists of a canvas tarp with a funnel in the middle.

Fig. 12-1 *Rain Catcher*

It has grommets all around the edge for convenient rigging anywhere on the boat. A garden hose is attached to the funnel and then led to the filler pipe on deck (or through a hatch or port) directly to your water tank. This rain catcher is easy to keep clean and free of salt spray, unlike a Bimini top, dodger, or awning, and folds up to stow nicely in any small place. We find that we can set it up permanently when we are moored at one place for a while, or, when we are sailing, we can rig it under the main boom to catch the rain as it runs through the drain in the boom and funnel it into the tanks. (It is, of course, important to let sufficient rain wash all salt out of the sail before beginning to catch water.

MATERIALS

- 6 yards treated canvas 36" wide
- 1 spool polyester thread
- 1 PVC pipe fiting (½" × ¼" insert coupling)
- 1 small stainless steel clamp to fit over pipe fitting
- 1 length of garden hose
- 1 light line, #4, ⅛"
- 8 grommets

CONSTRUCTION

Step 1. Cut 18" off the length of the material to use for the funnel.

Step 2. Cut the remaining length of cloth in half.

Step 3. Hem the long outside edges of both pieces.

Step 4. Place the two remaining long edges, right sides together, and sew with a flat felled seam.

Step 5. Make a funnel out of the extra 18". Roll it into funnel shape, and cut the excess material away. Sew the side seam and zigzag the raw edge. The top diameter should be at least 6", and the bottom diameter should be slightly larger than the PVC hose fitting.

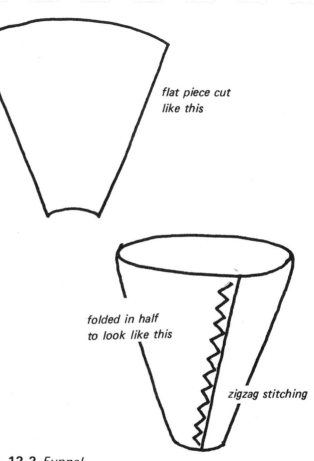

flat piece cut like this

folded in half to look like this

zigzag stitching

Fig. 12-2 *Funnel*

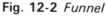

Step 6. Place the funnel on the very center of the main piece and trace lightly around it; or, measure a circle of the same circumference in that exact spot. Cut ½" in from the circle just drawn. This will provide a hole in the main piece 1" smaller in diameter than the funnel.

Step 7. Pin the funnel edge to the edge of the hole. Stitch around these edges three times, zigzagging the rough edges the third time around.

Step 8. Hem the ends of the rectangle.

Step 9. Place 8 grommets at the edges and corners of the panel.

Step 10. Insert the PVC fitting in the funnel and snug the cloth down tight on it with the hose clamp.

Step 11. Attach light line to the grommets where necessary to rig it low on the boat.

Step 12. Screw the garden hose to the PVC fitting and lead the other end of your hose to the tank filler and wait for rain.

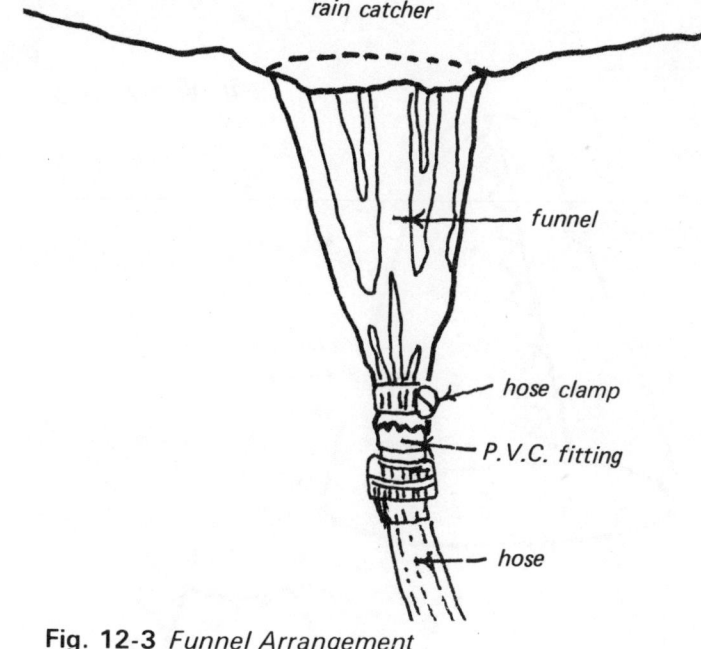

Fig. 12-3 *Funnel Arrangement*

The completed rain catcher can also be used as a small sun awning or waterproof cover when you are cruising in areas where you do not have to depend on rain for your water.

Chapter thirteen

A COVER FOR THE YACHT TENDER

Whether you're carrying a 25-foot runabout on the upper deck of a motor yacht or a 7-foot pram in davits, you will find that a cover will reduce maintenance time. A cover will protect varnish, gelcoat and upholstery from the damaging effects of sun, water and dirt. A cover can also convert a dinghy into an extra storage space. Gear usually associated with the tender such as life jackets, diving gear, water skis and gas tanks, can be stowed inside the tender when not in use. The cover keeps everything shipshape and dry. The size of the tender has less effect on the difficulty involved in making a cover than does the number of projections above its deck level, such as windshields or outboard motors.

MATERIALS

Treated canvas is the best cover material for tenders because it is waterproof. Acrylic canvas is not especially good for tender covers because it will allow water to leak through if puddles form. If a ridge pole, arched bows, or something similar, can be rigged to keep water from collecting, acrylic canvas can be used and it will outlast treated canvas.

Weblon is also a good material for tender covers. It is waterproof and easily scrubbed clean. A Weblon cover, however, that is left on a tender for long periods of time will cause condensation under the cover which will eventually cause mildew, unless some means of ventialtion is designed into the cover.

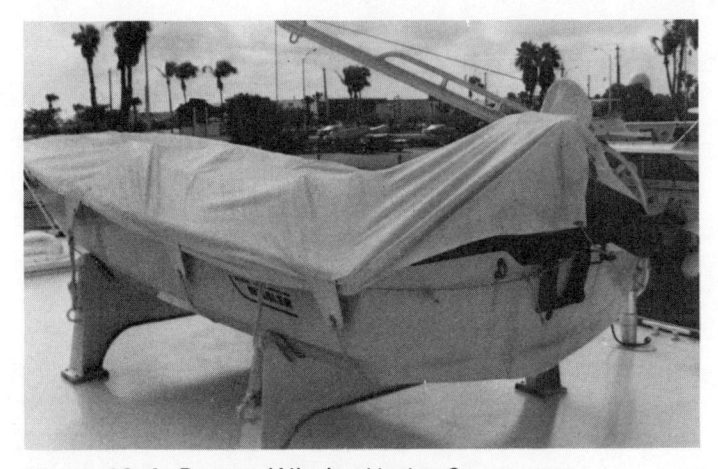

Photo 13-1 *Boston Whaler Under Cover*

Nylon sailcloth has been successfully used for tender covers but should not be expected to last very long as the sun will devour it.

Fastenings should be chosen before the cloth portion of the cover is designed. Small dinghies with overhanging gunwales may require only a cover held by a drawstring or shock cord threaded through a casing that runs all around the dinghy and snugs up under the gunwales. A larger tender with a windshield, motor or tow bar might need to have its cover snapped directly to the hull.

A cover will work more efficiently if an oar, boathook, mop, or a specially designed dowel or batten can be used for a ridge pole. This will reduce leakage in the cover and provide better ventilation. Such a pole can run from bow to stern, gunwale to gunwale, or stand vertically and poke through a grommeted hole in the cover. The position of the ridge pole or flexible batten should be designed into the cover at the time measurements are made.

MEASURING

Step 1. Measure the beam of the tender at key points so that the shape can be established. It is usually helpful also to measure the distance *between* these measurements. Place all measurements on a clear diagram.

Step 2. Measure the overall length of the tender and place on the diagram.

Step 3. Measure for windshields, etc. A paper pattern of the windshield curve and the area of the bow in front of the windshield is usually necessary for proper fit, and is definitely worth the slight extra work of making such a pattern.

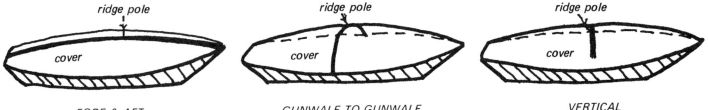

FORE & AFT GUNWALE TO GUNWALE VERTICAL

Fig. 13-2 *Rigging a Ridge Pole*

Step 4. Measure the extra length of material necessary to overlap the gunwale. Remember to add seam allowance and hem and/or casing allowance to each width measurement.

Photo 13-3 *Davits Used for Ridge Pole*

CONSTRUCTION

Step 1. Based on your measurements, decide whether it is more advantageous to run the cloth panels fore and aft on the tender or athwartship. Most covers are made with the panels sewn in strips from gunwale to gunwale. Decide how many panels it will take to cover the boat, and how long each one should be. For instance, if panels will run athwartship and your cloth is 36" wide, measure 35" forward from the stern, less hem allowance, and see what the width should be. Cut the first panel, remembering to allow for seams and hems. Then measure 35" forward from the last "station" (seam between panels), and check for the greatest width necessary within that 35". Continue to measure and cut these panels until you have enough of them to cover the tender.

Step 2. Sew these panels together with flat felled seams.

Step 3. Using the paper patterns you have made of the windshield (if any) and the curve of the windshield where it attaches to the foredeck, cut the piece of cloth that will cover the windshield. Then, with the foredeck pattern, cut the curve into the aftermost edge of the foredeck section of the cover. Sew the windshield piece to the foredeck section. Then sew the rest of the panels to the top of the windshield piece.

If an outboard motor cover is part of the tender cover, it is usually made with two side pieces and a strip that covers the front, top and back of the motor. It should be sewn together first and then sewn into the tender cover. Usually a drawstring that goes around the stern half of the motor is required to keep this portion of the cover securely on the motor.

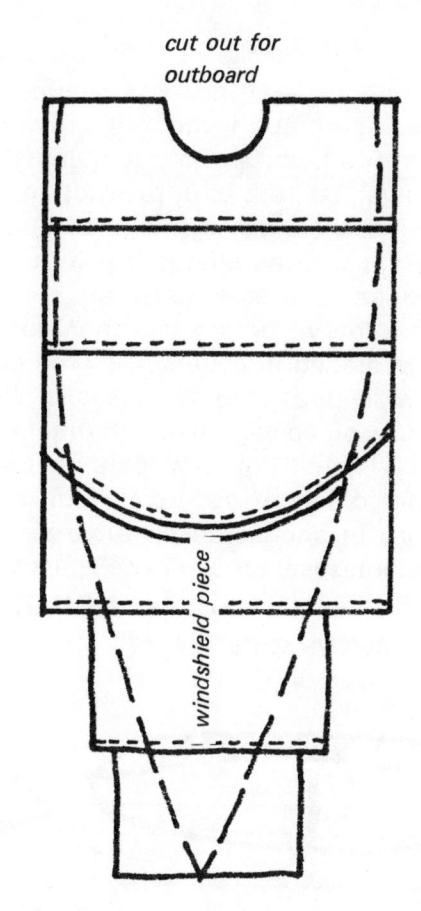

cut out for outboard

windshield piece

Fig. 13-4 *Panels of Tender Cover with Windshield and Outboard Inserted*

Step 4. Place the cover over the tender and mark the outside edge all around the boat so that it will fasten where you want it to. Then, allowing a 2" hem, or a 3" casing if using a drawstring, cut the shape of the cover. If there is a considerable curvature allow 4" of hem. Then cut 3½" of that hem off and use it as a tabling to be sewn to the cover in place of a hem. This will keep puckers and darts to a minimum. Mark cutouts for cleats or chocks that might be used with the cover in place.

Step 5. Hem the outside, being careful to match the measurements exactly, or sew a casing around the outside. If using a tabling, first sew the raw edges of the tabling strip by folding over ¼" and stitching. Then fold the tabling strip in half and place over the outside edge of the cover. Stitch through all three thicknesses at once. Be sure to match the tabling to the place it was cut from on the cover and stitch around the edge twice. Stitch, cut and finish the necessary cutouts. (*Refer to Chapter 4*)

Photo 13-5 *Beautifully-Made Cover with Cutouts for Cleats*

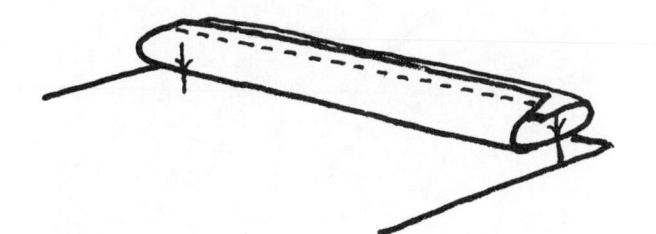

Fig. 13-6 *Tabling the Edge of the Cover*

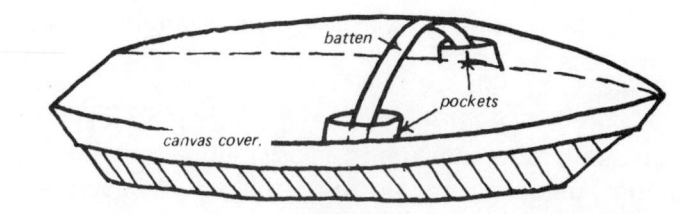

Fig. 13-7 *Ridge Pole Pockets*

Step 6. Make pockets for ridge pole if necessary. For instance, a horizontal ridge pole could have pockets at either side of the cover to hold the pole and force it to bend.

Step 7. Attach fastenings. If you are using snaps, *first* attach them to the boat and *then* to the cover. They will need to be placed every 8″ to 10″ apart. A drawstring can be inserted with a safety pin and worked through the casing.

Step 8. Fit the cover to the tender and test it on the first really windy day to make sure it cannot be blown off.

Photo 13-8 *Dinghy Cover Fastened with Tie-Downs and Shock Cord*

92

Chapter fourteen

FITTED SHEETS AND PILLOWCASES

Making fitted sheets for your boat's berths is a simple task, and the sheets will ease the daily chore of bed-making. Fitted sheets also reduce the lumps and bumps caused by the excess sheet and blanket tucked under the usually odd-shaped mattress. All that is required to make fitted sheets are a bit of elastic, some thread, and sheets to cut down—either sheets you already own or new ones. If you buy new sheets, consider the large king- and queen-size sheets as well as those closest to the size of your berth. Sometimes it is possible and economical to get two boat sheets out of one large sheet, and with little waste. Don't throw away any scraps: At very least they make good rags, and we have occasionally even been able to make draperies or pillow slips from leftover scraps.

93

MATERIALS

Sheets to be cut down for each berth
12″ of ¼″ flat elastic to sew around each corner
of each sheet
Polyester thread

CONSTRUCTION

Bottom Sheets

Step 1. Lay the sheet right side up, over the mattress to be fitted. Mark the place where the top mattress corners hit the sheet with a pin.

Step 2. At each corner pin in the dart that will be made.

For outside corners greater than 90 degrees make darts as marked or simply cut a curve around the corner, and the elastic will take up the slack.

For an inside corner, leave enough slack material for the sheet to cover it. It will take more cloth than an outside corner or the sheet will not tuck under the mattress.

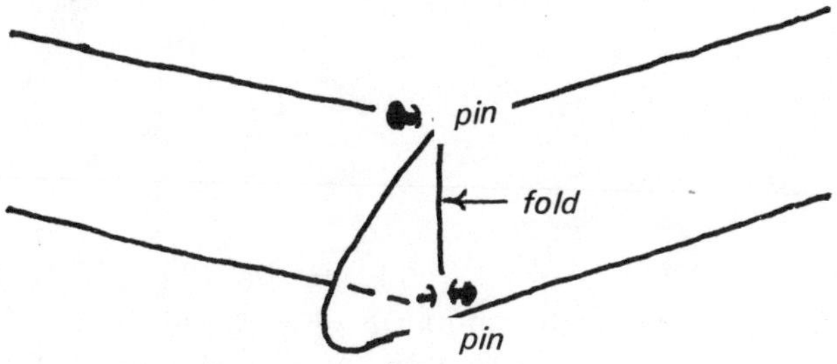

Fig. 14-1 *Pinning the Dart*

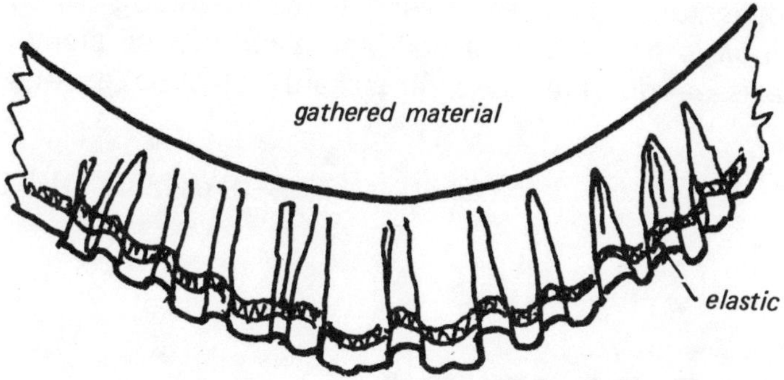

Fig. 14-2 *Making a Greater than 90-degree Corner*

94

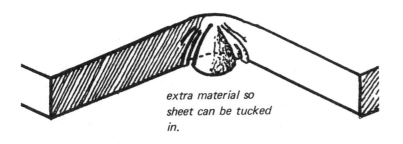

extra material so
sheet can be tucked
in.

Fig. 14-3 *Inside Corner*

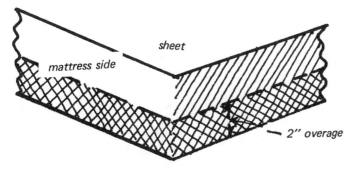

sheet

mattress side

— 2" overage

Fig. 14-4 *Sides of the Sheet*

Step 3. Cut off the excess material. Be sure to leave enough material to cover the sides of the mattress, plus 2".

Step 4. Stitch the darts and cut off excess material. Hem the outside edges you have cut, using a small rolled hem.

Step 5. Cut pieces of elastic 12" long to sew to each corner. If one end of the sheet is only 20" or so long, cut one piece of elastic to sew around the entire end.

Step 6. Pin one end of the elastic 10" away from the corner along the end edge, and the other end of the elastic 10" away from the corner along the side edge.

Step 7. Begin sewing at one end, stretching the elastic as you sew. The elastic should stretch enough so that the sheet remains flat until after the presser foot has passed over it. Then the elastic will relax and gather the sheet.

Step 8. Repeat Steps 6 and 7 for all corners.

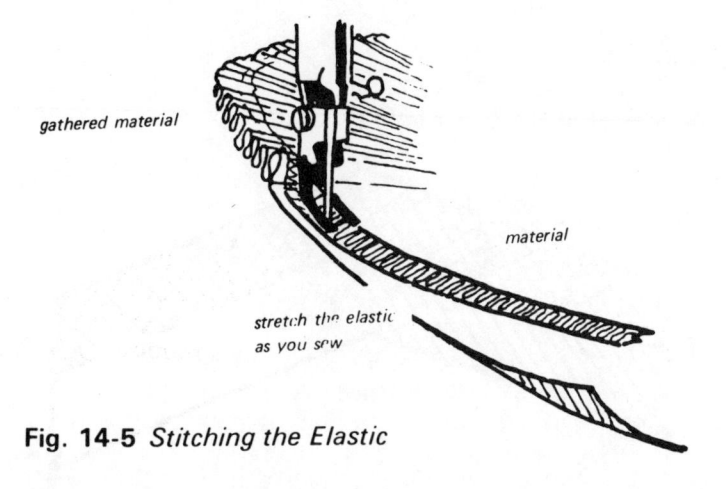

Fig. 14-5 *Stitching the Elastic*

gathered material

material

stretch the elastic
as you sew

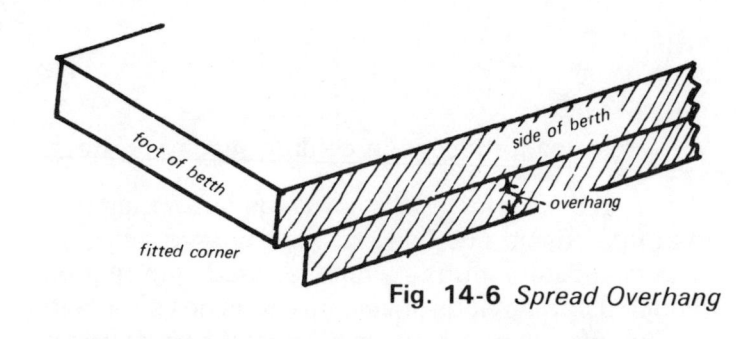

foot of berth

side of berth

overhang

fitted corner

Fig. 14-6 *Spread Overhang*

Top Sheets and Blankets

Measure top sheets and blankets the same way you measured the bottom sheet, but make corners at the foot only. The sides of the top sheets and blankets should be left at least 8″ wider than the mattress on both sides to allow a person to roll over and still be covered. Hem the sides and make the corners at the foot of the sheets as you did for the bottom sheets. The head of the sheet will have been hemmed by the factory.

Blankets can be cut and fitted at the bottom exactly like sheets. Blanket-binding tape can be purchased from any cloth store to bind the edges. Fold this binding over the raw edge of the blanket and stitch through all three thicknesses at once.

Bedspreads

Quilts or heavy-fabric spreads can also be fitted. It is often desirable to allow a spread to hang slightly over the edge of the berth. In this case, take very small darts at the foot of the spread and cut the extra overhang from that point. Half-inch elastic might be preferable at the corners of very heavy material.

A V-berth can be finished nicely with one spread for both berths. Place the spread you are cutting

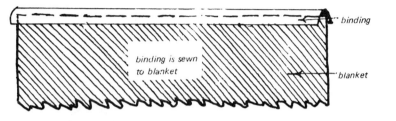
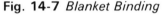

Fig. 14-7 *Blanket Binding*

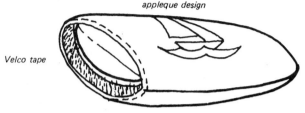

Fig. 14-8 *Case-Type Cover with Velcro*

down or adequate cloth over the V-berth cushions. Mark the outside corners at the foot of the berth and make darts. Place elastic around the entire end. Put the spread back on the cushions and mark the inside, outside and head of the spread. Allow for the side edge and a 2" overlap as you did with the sheets. Cut the cloth and hem all around the edges. Finish the inside edge with blanket binding or bias tape of a matching or contrasting color.

Pillowcases and Bolster Covers

Pillowcases or bolster covers that match or complement your upholstery or bedspread make an attractive addition to your vessel's beauty and comfort. A pillowcase also allows you to use a sleeping pillow for lounging without soiling the pillow, and,

because it fits in with your decor, it eliminates the need to stow the sleeping pillow in a locker during the day.

The simplest pillowcase to make is a copy of a regular pillowcase, made of matching or contrasting fabric and fastened with snaps or Velcro tape at the open end. A pattern can be made from a regular pillowcase. Appliques, embroidery, needlepoint and monogramming can be used to dress it up if desired.

Another method of making a pillowcase requires no fastening. This type of pillowcase has overlap-edges and works best with small prints or plain material that doesn't require matching. First cut a piece of fabric long enough and wide enough to fit the pillow with the overlap. Hem both ends with a narrow hem. Fold the cloth wrong side out so that

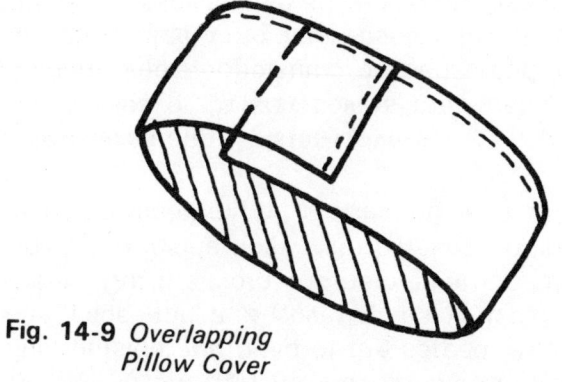

Fig. 14-9 *Overlapping Pillow Cover*

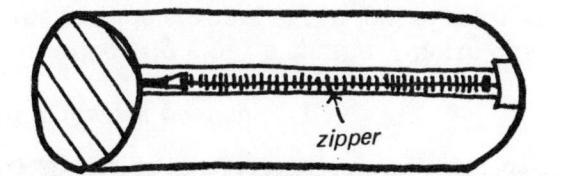

zipper

Fig. 14-10 *Bolster Pillow Cover*

it matches the size of the pillow and overlaps on one side, and pin. Sew the pillowcase up both sides with the right sides together. Turn right side out.

A bolster-type pillow case is another nice way to stow extra pillows used only when guests are a-board. Such bolsters can also be used to stow bedding that is not often needed and is difficult to stow. A round bolster is constructed exactly like a duffel bag, but without handles. For more complete instructions refer to Chapter 6. To make a simple bolster, roll up the pillow or bedding the way you would like it to be in its finished shape. Measure the diameter and circumference of the roll and the overall length. Cut two circles to match the diameter, one for each end, and one length of cloth to match the circumference and the overall length for the main piece. Remember to add seam allowances and hems. Put in the zipper as Chapter 6 describes —a dressmaker's long dress zipper will usually do— and stitch in the end pieces. Turn the bolster right side out, and there you have a wonderful bolster for your weary back and stowage for your pillows or bedding.

Chapter fifteen

CUSHIONS

Interior and exterior cushions do much to add to the beauty and comfort of a vessel. Their placement, size and fabric will directly affect their usefulness and durability. They are well worth careful planning.

INTERIOR CUSHIONS

Foam: Interior cushions can be made with any type of foam, but polyurethane foam is the most readily available and will not rot or disintegrate if it gets wet, as foam rubber will. Polyurethane foam is available in different densities, which are referred to in terms of firmness. Soft foam is rarely used on boats because there is usually not room aboard for the thickness needed to achieve a comfortable seat. It can, however, be used effectively for seat backs that you plan to "tuft" with buttons. Medium-density foam is normally found on boats in 3" to 4" thicknesses, although it is most comfortable when it is 4" to 6" thick. Medium-density foam may "bottom out" after a few years of hard use. Cushions that will be slept on, or seats that allow for only a few inches of foam thickness should be made with high-density polyurethane foam. It will not be as soft to sit on as the medium-density but it will "bottom out" less and keep its resiliency longer.

99

Placement And Size: The placement and size of interior cushions are usually dictated by the existing berths or "chairs" in the vessel. A few comments are in order, however, if you are building, re-designing or modifying your boat interior.

Cushions obviously can be placed or scattered anywhere you sit or lie, but they can also be used as backrests and head pillows. The standard transom berth arrangement found on many sailboats is the boat's main seating area. Backrests here are much more comfortable than locker doors. Cushions can be designed to snap on to locker doors and open with them, or can be designed to snap on above the lockers and hinge up for access to the lockers. In this second case the cushion back itself can serve as the locker door.

Bulkheads at the ends of berths are rarely cushioned, yet they often are the natural backrests, where crew members like to lean and read. Why not snap a permanent cushion there? Steps or levels are often found in small cabins on boats. The triangular bin between V-berths immediately comes to mind. Cushioned, such spaces make nice places to sit while putting on your shoes. V-berths are often not well cushioned. The foam should be higher than the fiddle

Photo 15-1 *Corner Settee*

or sea rail to prevent bruised shins and fannies. Often the foot of a V-berth would be improved by the additon of a cushion on the forward bulkhead—to lean against while reading. There are many places aboard where a cushion placed against the inner hull lining produces a cozy corner for relaxing.

Fabric

Vinyl: A few years ago the only fabric used in boats was vinyl. It was easy to maintain and would absorb

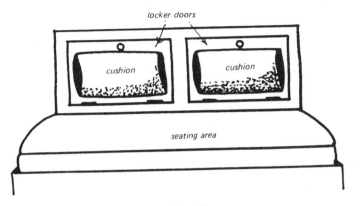

locker doors

cushion

cushion

seating area

Fig. 15-2 *Backrests on Locker Doors*

much wear without showing it. That is still largely true. Stains and spilled food can be wiped off vinyl with a damp sponge. Sea water has little effect on it and it does not scuff or tear easily. But you will damage vinyl if you drop a hot match or cigarette on it; it *does* melt. The only drawback to vinyl is its non-porous, plastic quality. It is sticky to sit on in hot weather. Most people find it intolerable to sleep on without a thick matress pad between the vinyl and their skin.

Canvas bottoms can be used in vinyl cushions that cannot, because of their odd shape, be flipped over. The canvas will make drying out the cushion, if it gets wet, an easy matter, and will save money as it is less expensive than vinyl.

Herculon: Herculon is being used more and more on boats. It is a good second choice to vinyl as far as wearability is concerned. Herculon and similar brands are woven polyester materials that have a latex backing, and allow a larger variety of color and pattern than vinyl. Herculon comes in solids, stripes, tweeds, plaids and floral designs, and makes beautiful cushions. Some of it feels a bit scratchy on bare skin, but it is not sticky. Its drawbacks, however, deserve some thought: It stretches rather easily and it will snag; stains may be difficult to remove from it, especially after the Scotchgarding has worn off.

Treated Canvas: Treated canvas is by far the most comfortable fabric to sit on that is also practical for boats. It is cool and soft in hot weather, and warm and cozy in cold weather. It is available in a few colors and stripes. However, it does stain easily. It must be washed and dried to preshrink it before it is made up

101

into cushions; even then the next washing may cause it to shrink more.

Corduroy and Others: A good quality corduroy will make comfortable cushions and will wear fairly well. Corduroy will not last as long as canvas, though, and it has the same drawbacks. Loosely woven materials such as linen or synthetic linen are not suitable for use on boats. Besides staining, fraying, fading and snagging, loosely woven cloth will not hold its shape. You are better off to stick to heavier fabrics that have been given some sort of water resistant treatment.

Quality: In fabrics, as in any other product, there are name brands. You do not have to buy "Naugahyde" vinyl to get good vinyl, but look for the quality of "Naugahyde" vinyl. The vinyl should be thick and pliable with a closely woven cloth backing. If it is thin and has a cheesecloth-type backing, don't buy it. The same is true when you shop for Herculon. There are other latex-backed fabrics as good or better. But look for a smooth, even coating of latex and closely woven fibers. If the backing is lumpy, chances are the cloth has been inconsistently woven and coated and will wear out more quickly than a better grade. Quality material will more than pay for its extra cost as it will

make up more easily, look better and wear longer. It takes time to make cushion covers properly and they should not have to be replaced frequently.

CUSHIONS FOR OUTSIDE USE

Foam: Polyurethane foam is very good for use outdoors. It will not rot from moisture and will not disintegrate as mentioned above. It is also much lighter than foam rubber. Unicellular or closed-cell foam is even better because it will not absorb water. This type foam is quite expensive, but will last a very long time outdoors. Thickness and density, as in interior cushions, will depend on the space and the intended use of the cushion, as defined earlier.

Placement: The placement of exterior cushions is often important not only for comfort but also for the safety of the vessel. It's not a good idea to place cushions where they might foul gear or cause someone to slip or trip. Make sure cushions in the cockpit fit the seating space exactly, yet do not interfere with travelers, blocks or steering gear. If the space you wish to cover is irregular, make a paper pattern to get the shape accurately before you start. If the cushions are placed where they could blow away in the wind, such as on the foredeck, use strong snaps to hold them down.

Size: The size of your exterior cushions obviously will be dictated by the size of your seating arrangement. However, if you want to stow the cushions below during bad weather or when you're away from the vessel, making two small cushions to fit one long seat will make stowage and handling easier. Small cushions often fit in several alternate locations in your boat.

Fabric: Vinyl, for the reasons stated above, is the best choice for exterior cushions. It is really the only fabric that can stand the heavy wear that cockpit cushions normally receive. We suggest that a treated canvas bottom be placed in the bottom of each cushion. This allows a wet cushion to be flipped over and dried quickly in the sun. Canvas will also give you a cooler, softer side to sit on in extremely hot weather. It will get dirty, however, so it is best to put canvas on the bottom only. Cushion covers made of all canvas only will look terrible in a few months.

MATERIALS

Fabric: Have enough fabric to cover the top and bottom of each cushion, plus enough pieces of fabric 1″ wider than the thickness of the cushion, to go around all the sides of the cushion, plus enough 1½″ strips to make cording. Both top and bottom edges of the cushion should be corded if they will show or can be flipped over. If there is a retaining fiddle or lip that will hide the bottom edge of the cushion, the bottom edge need not be corded.

Zippers: Have a zipper long enough to run along the longest *hidden* side of each cushion. Delrin zipper tape is the best. Because it is plastic, it will not rust, and even if a few teeth are missing, the zipper will still work. Buy the number of yards of material needed to do the whole job, and cut each length as you need it. Buy the sliders separately and slip them on yourself. The sides of the fabric are sewn in such a manner as to act as a stop for the zipper; you will not need to buy stops. Delrin zipper tape comes in two sizes, 5-D and 10-D. The smaller, 5-D, is adequate for cushions.

Cording String: Number 4 twine or nylon line is best for cording. Nylon is best for exterior cushions but not absolutely necessary. Buy enough cording to do the whole job; you might want to make up all of it in one session.

Thread: Polyester thread works well on all fabrics. Make sure that you are sewing with a long stitch length on vinyl as too many needle holes may cause vinyl to tear.

CONSTRUCTION

Cutting The Foam: If you are not using foam already cut to size or you cannot get the dealer to cut it for you, carefully mark the individual cushions on the sheet of foam with a felt-tip pen. For simple rectangles and squares, ruler measurements will suffice (but do them carefully: measure *twice* before you mark and cut). For irregular shapes, it is best to make a paper pattern first, check it against the location, *then* mark and cut the foam. A serrated knife, electric carving knife or handsaw will cut the foam easily. With the serrated knife, use a lot of sawing action and very little pressure. Slow smooth strokes make a clean cut.

Planning Extra Ties Or Snap Tabs: If a cushion needs to be snapped to a bulkhead or seat, or be tied around a chair, plan for snap tab locations first. Measure how long they should be and label the edge of the material to which they will be sewn. A snap tab will usually need to be 1½" wide, so cut a strip 3½" wide and the required length, hem the ends of the strip, fold it in half and stitch it together. There is no need to finish the raw edges because they will be inside the cushion seam. When you stitch the side piece to the bottom of the cushion, be sure to insert this tab into the proper seam and stitch through all thicknesses. Ties should be made the same way except that their raw edges *should* be finished.

Cutting The Fabric:

Step 1. *Top and Bottom:* Roll the fabric out on a large flat surface. Arrange to cut the tops and bottoms along one edge of the piece of fabric and leave the remaining edge for the long side pieces. Mark all the pieces before cutting, and label them. Write only in the seam allowance, or use pencil or tailor's chalk. Felt-tip pen markings will eventually bleed through the fabric. Label the sides where the zippers go. Label tops and bottoms. The easiest and most exact way to mark the cloth is with the foam cushion itself, after it has been cut to fit the required space. Place the cushion on the wrong side of the fabric. Trace around the outside edge of the cushion with a pencil or tailor's chalk. Do this with all the pieces of foam until you've marked all the tops and bottoms you'll need. (Sides are based on foam thickness plus seam allowance.)

Step 2. *Sides:* In order to find the total amount of material needed for your project measure the circumference of each cushion. Add all these circumferences together, then add a 3" allowance for seams and for finishing the zipper on each cushion. If your fabric length allows, it is desirable to have one continuous side piece go all around each cushion. The next best choice is to have one piece the length of the zipper side of the cushion and one piece that will go around the other three sides. Sometimes, because of the length of your material, you will have to sew the side pieces together to get the required length. So if your foam is 4" thick, mark enough 5" (½" seam allowances) pieces to go around all of your cushions.

Step 3. *Cording:* Mark off enough 1½" cording strips to do all of your cording. Cording strips cut from woven fabrics without backing should be cut on the bias. Backed fabrics, such as vinyl and Herculon can be cut on the straight of the goods.

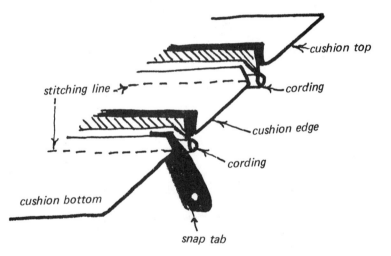

Fig. 15-3 *Inserting the Snap Tab*

105

Step 4. Cut out the tops and bottoms of the cushion covers *just outside* your traced line of the cushion shape. You should make the covers a tight fit or they will wrinkle and bag. By cutting the pieces the same shape as the cushion and then sewing ½" inside that line you will get a good snug fit. Cut the side pieces and cording strips as you have marked them.

Step 5. Arrange all of the pieces for each cushion in piles to keep the pieces organized. Don't forget extra tabs and ties if they are to be used. Now stitch the side pieces end-to-end if necessary to get proper length, and sew in the tabs and ties where needed.

Cording the Side Piece

Step 6. The cording string can be sewn into the cording strips as they are being sewn onto the side pieces. Take a cording strip and fold it over the cording so that the edges of the strip match up. When using unbacked woven fabrics cut on the bias, the cording strips should first be sewn together to produce the required length. Place strips right side together and sew a ¼" seam. Vinyl and backed fabrics will not unravel, and pieces can be added as the cord is sewn into the strips.

slide this piece over piece to be joined

stitching

Fig. 15-4 *Joining Cording Strips*

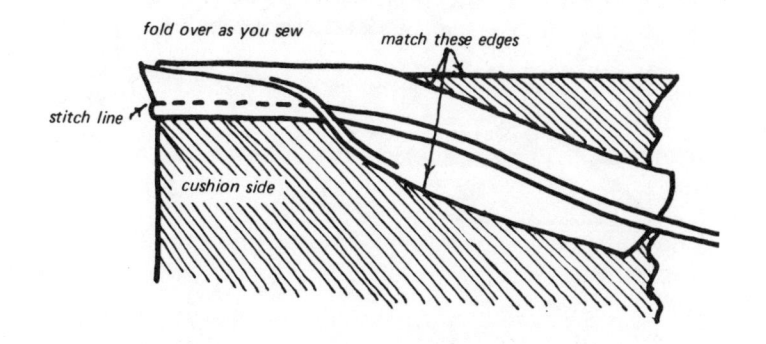

fold over as you sew

match these edges

stitch line

cushion side

Fig. 15-5 *Sewing the Cording to the Side Strip*

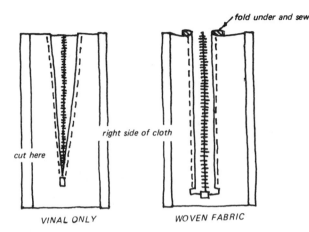

fold under and sew

right side of cloth

cut here

VINAL ONLY   WOVEN FABRIC

Fig. 15-6 *Finishing Off the Zipper*

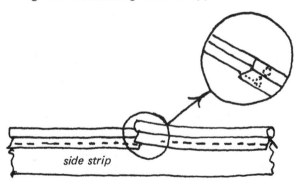

side strip

Fig. 15-7 *Overlapping the Cording*

Match the edges of the cording strip with the edge of the side piece. This should give you a ½" seam allowance if you sew through the strip right up against the cord. Using the zipper foot in your machine, sew both the top and bottom cording onto this strip. Leave the last few inches of cording strip and side piece unstitched for overlapping later.

Zipper

Step 7. Starting at one end of the side piece, place the zipper face down in the center of the wrong side of the piece. Stitch the zipper in the middle of the side piece, sewing close to the *outside* edge of the zipper tape. Stitch down one side of the zipper and then up the other, lock-stitching both ends of the seams. Now turn the side piece so that the right side is facing you. With a ripper or scissors make a cut in the cloth directly over the center of the zipper. If you are using vinyl, the zipper is finished. If you are using woven fabric, roll the raw edge of the cloth under, next to the zipper, and stitch down both sides. This "buries" the raw edge of the cut opening in the side piece, and puts a second line of stitching in the zipper, making for a stronger job.

107

Sewing the Side Piece to the Top

Step 8. Place the right side of the zipper end of the side piece next to the right side of the top along the edge to be zippered. Line up the edges and begin stitching 3" in from the beginning of the side piece. Stitch the side piece to the top all the way around, staying tight against the cording with the zipper foot. When you reach the beginning of the side piece, cut the excess strip away, but leave enough to fold under 2" of the end to finish the raw edge. Tuck this folded edge under the zipper end of the side piece. Cut out ½" of cord and cut the cording strip. Lap the cordless end of the cording strip over the other end of the cording and stitch through all thicknesses. (Refer to Chapter 4 for making cushion corners.) If your machine can't handle this much thickness at once, sew the last few inches by hand.

Stitch the end edges of the side piece together, overlapping the cording as you did on the top.

Sewing in the Bottom

Step 9. Unzip the zipper half way. Make small slashes in the bottom edge of the side piece directly above the corners made in the top. This will locate exactly where to make the bottom corner. Stitch the bottom onto the side piece, right sides together, just as you did the top. Turn the cushion right side out. As you sew, make sure that all corners are strong and that you are consistently close

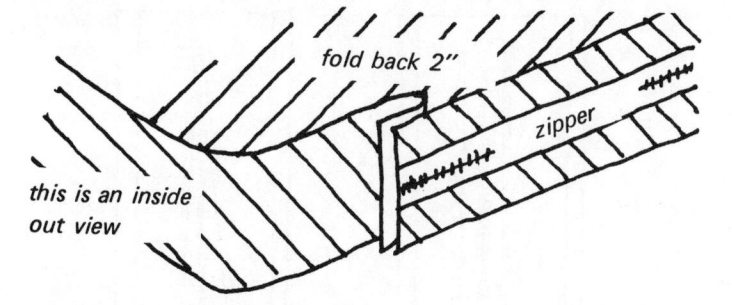

fold back 2"

zipper

this is an inside out view

Fig. 15-8 *Finishing the End of the Side Strip*

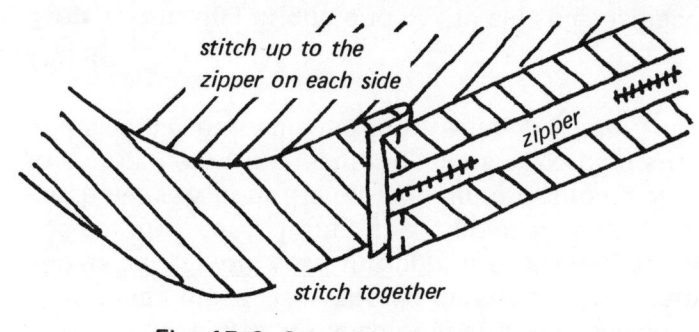

stitch up to the zipper on each side

zipper

stitch together

Fig. 15-9 *Stitching the Ends of the Side Strip*

to the cording. Go back and restitch any places that don't look just right. Put the foam carefully into the cover, working it into the far corners, and zip it up. Small corners of the cover that are slightly too large can be stuffed with shredded foam. The next one you make will be easier.

COVERING A SETTEE BACK

If you have the type of settee with the back made of plywood, you can recover it easily.

Step 1. Remove the back from the settee and remove the staples and buttons, if any. Cut a piece of fabric that will cover the back generously. If the back is curved, note how the darts were made in the old cover and duplicate them in the new piece of cloth.

Step 2. Using bronze or Monel staples (because they don't rust), stretch the new piece of cloth over the foam and around to the back side of the plywood. Begin at the top edge. Staple from the middle toward the outside edges, making sure to pull the material snug. Then do the bottom edge, again starting at the center and pulling the material down

and out toward the ends. The side edges are the most difficult. Make neatly pleated corners and stretch the fabric tightly over the ends, but do not depress the foam any more in one spot than you have elsewhere.

BUTTONS

It is often advisable to button cushions that are used as backrests. This will keep the material from sagging downward when people slouch against the cushions, and also give the cushions a bit of an over-stuffed look.

MATERIALS

Covered buttons
Plastic backing buttons
Strong marline or Dacron cord (waxed)
Long sail needle

CONSTRUCTION

Step 1. Cover the buttons. Button forms for covering can be purchased at most dry goods stores. There are two types: The best type has the attaching ring on the

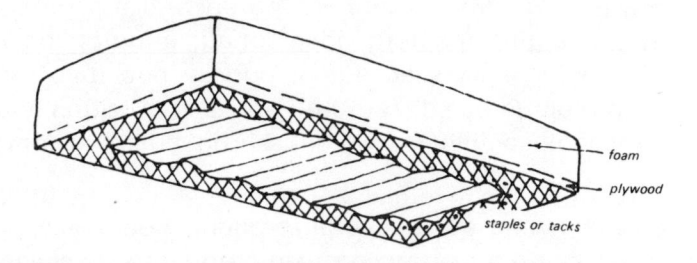

Fig. 15-10 *Covering a Settee Back*

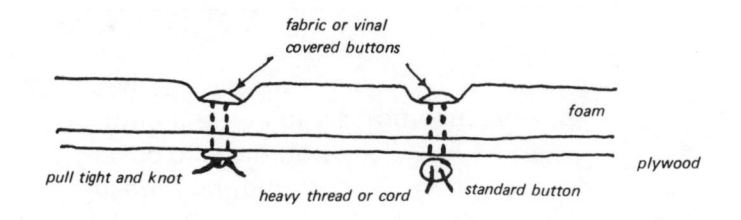

Fig. 15-11 *Buttoning*

button side rather than on the back. Buttons with the attaching ring on the back tend to pull apart. If you are using vinyl, strip off the laminate from the back if you can. This will reduce thickness and make the button easier to cover.

Step 2. Mark the positions of the buttons on the back of the cushion or plywood. Drill a small hole for each button in the plywood.

Step 3. With a 2' length of heavy waxed cord, thread the sail needle. Put the needle through one side of the plastic backing button, then through the back of the cushion. Depress the foam until you can reach the needle. Pull the thread through until you have 2" to 3" left below the backing button. Feed the needle through the covered button and back through the cushion and backing button. Pull the threads so that the covered button depresses the foam and tie a good square knot on top of the backing button. Continue this procedure with all of the buttons, being careful in each case to depress the foam no more and no less than you did with the first button.

110

Chapter sixteen

CURTAINS

Curtains aboard any vessel should be functional, practical and attractive. Whether you are closing out the night and the people in the next slip, or dividing the forward head from the forward cabin, a curtain does not provide privacy if you can see through, under or around it. Neither is it desirable for the curtain to float on the wind from an open port or sway out and in with the motion of the boat. It is necessary, therefore, to design boat curtains that are securely fastened and easily opened and closed. It is also important to make them of a material that is washable, resistant to water staining and mildew, and retains its shape. The hardware used to hang and fasten the curtains should be rust-proof: brass, stainless steel, plastic or aluminum.

Fabric
Most synthetic fabrics such as nylon, polyester, Dacron and fiberglass wear well aboard boats. Before buying material, be sure to check the fabric for washing instructions. As most curtains aboard will often be wet or damp, it is impractical to have to dry clean them. Polyester and cotton blends are excellent for the hardiest curtains but may limit your choice of pattern and texture.

Unless you are an experienced sewer, choose a

pattern or texture that does not have to be matched. A plaid pattern or a horizontal stripe will require matching the patterns on one curtain with the next. You will need about one-third more cloth if you choose a pattern that must be matched. As you probably know, light colors tend to enlarge a space, dark colors to shrink it. Stripes lengthen the space in the direction they flow. Very small patterns shrink a room as much as large patterns.

Lining Fabric

Woven cloth that looks the same or nearly the same on both sides may not have to be lined. If lining isn't necessary to darken the curtained area, this type of fabric is a wonderful choice, as lining curtains is difficult and expensive. However, if your chosen material rots in sunlight, you may save money in the long run by lining the curtains with a sun-resistant fabric. There are also synthetic linings that are coated with a rubbery latex to keep water from reaching the drapery fabric and also to act as a total sun screen. For large saloon windows this lining is probably a good investment.

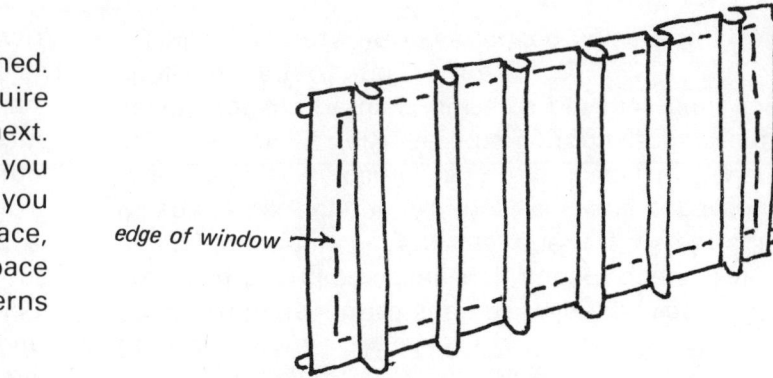

edge of window

Fig. 16-1 *Pleated Drapes, Fastened Top and Bottom*

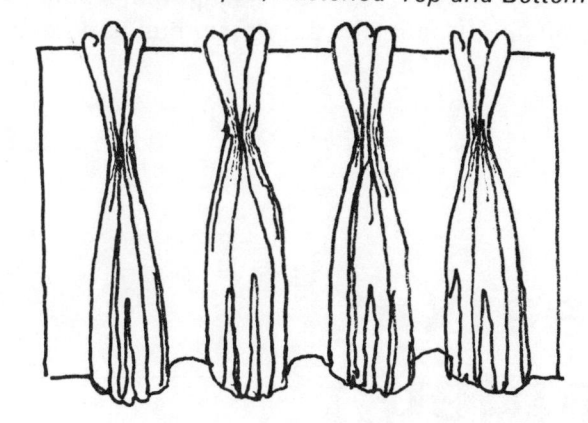

Fig. 16-2 *Pleated Drapes (Traditional)*

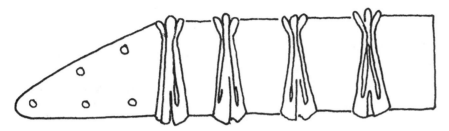

Fig. 16-3 *Flat-Corner Drape*

Fig. 16-5 *Shower Cap Curtain*

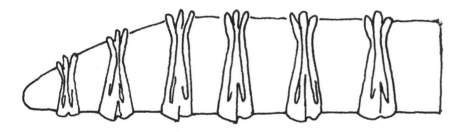

Fig. 16-4 *Pleated-Corner Drape*

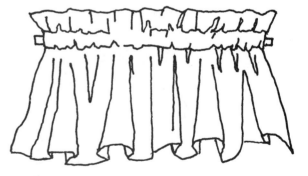

Fig. 16-6 *Casement Curtain over Forward Windows*

113

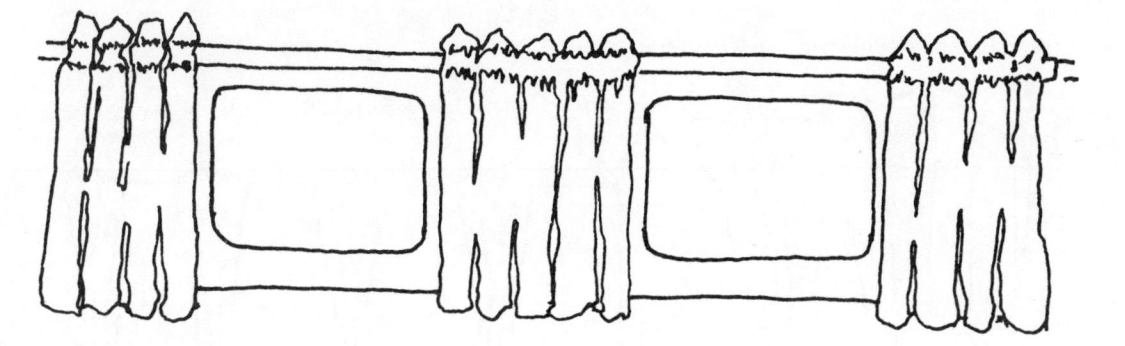

Fig. 16-7 *Casing Curtains*

Shape

Shape as well as color and texture should be carefully considered before buying fabric. Large saloon windows in power yachts can be curtained in many fashions, but the most functional style is the pleated drape that follows the window shape and fastens at the top and bottom of the window.

If the boat is rarely used in rough seas, a traditional pleated drape can be used without fastening to the bottom of the window.

Beware of large windows. They may seem to be parallel to the cabin sole or overhead but often are not. Careful measuring will be necessary to achieve an even hem.

Corner windows on power yachts have often been covered with a flat drape.

A more attractive drape can be made by pleating the angle as well.

Shirred drapes can be used to cover the forward windows of the saloon.

114

Round or oval ports can be covered with a "shower cap" type of curtain. This can be slipped over the port when privacy is desired and easily stowed when not needed.

Cabin sides with a row of ports that open can be curtained with traditional casing curtains. They can be closed when the port is closed or slid to the side when the ports are open. These curtains can have rods at the top and bottom.

Variations of the casing curtain can be used to cover lockers, doorways and hatches.

Tie-backs

Tie-backs should be used whenever a curtain is longer than 15" and is not fastened at the bottom. The tie-backs will restrict the motion of the curtain and keep it shipshape.

PREPARING THE FABRIC

The secret to well-hung drapes that do not sag or hang unevenly is cutting the panels exactly "on grain." There are two sets of threads that make up a woven fabric: the *warp* that runs lengthwise, and the *weft* that runs crosswise. The warp threads should par-allel the selvage of the fabric. These threads are usually stronger than the weft threads and so most curtain panels are cut along the lengthwise grain. Be sure that all the warp and weft threads in your fabric run at right angles to each other or your curtains will sag. If a fabric is treated with a soil-release or permanent-press finish, you will not be able to straighten the grain of the fabric. In this case, be sure that the pattern is printed "on grain" before buying the fabric. An off-grain pattern cannot be matched.

If the fabric is not labeled "preshrunk," clean the fabric before you cut it in exactly the way you intend to clean it in the future, i.e., wash in warm water and tumble dry. This should insure that any shrinking will take place before the curtains are cut.

Finding the grain is the next step. If the fabric can be torn without pulling the threads off grain, snip the selvage about 1" deep and tear the fabric with a quick pull right across to the opposite selvage edge. If the cloth will not tear, snip the selvage edge until you can pick up one or two crosswise threads and pull these threads gently until you create a "line" to the opposite selvage edge. Then cut along this thread "line" from selvage to selvage. Plaids can be straightened by cutting across the material on the edge of a bold crosswise stripe. If none of the above methods will work, ravel the edge of the cloth until one thread can be pulled all the way out. One of these methods will give you the first straight edge for cutting the panels of the curtains. Careful measurement from this first straight edge should keep you "on grain" for the rest of the panels. If you're not sure, rip another straight grain thread before you cut each panel.

MEASUREMENTS

Length

Measure each window or port that you are going to curtain. They may look alike but often are not. (Right angles on boats are hard to find.) Where do you want the curtain to stop—just above the covering board, just below the sill? What will your fasteners do to the length of the curtain? If they will lower it, be sure to take that into account when figuring length. Pleater hooks raise the curtain, so be sure to add extra length if you are going to use them. Casement curtains will rise a bit when the rod is inserted, so remember to make them a little longer than the measurement indicates. A standard hem for casing curtains is 2", and 3" or 4" hems are usually used on pleated drapes. If you are not lining the curtains, a 3" hem must be made at the top of a casing curtain, and a 4" hem on the top of pleated drapes unless you are using pleater tape. A ½" hem is sufficient with pleater tape.

Width

Casing curtains or cafe curtains should be at least half again as wide as the area that they are to cover. An attractive curtain will result if the curtain panel is twice as wide as the window or port. Pleated curtains traditionally use fabric panels three times the width of the window, but they will also be attractive at just twice the width. Try to plan the panels of wide drapes so that they are somewhat symmetrical. A ½" seam is enough between panels, and 1" or 2" should be allowed for side hems.

IRONING

When making any type of curtain, use a steam iron before you stitch anything. Careful measurement as you press in hems and seams will give you perfect curtains. For instance, after the panels have been sewn together, press the seam allowances open and flat. Then press in the top-edge hem. If you want a 2" hem, measure exactly 2" all the way along the top, fold over that amount and press. Then do the bottom edge the same way. Check the overall length of the curtain. Finally, press the side hems and then begin stitching. The same procedure should be followed with the lining of each curtain.

CASING CURTAINS

Casing curtains are the easiest to make and many times, aboard ship, the most practical. After preparing the fabric and cutting the necessary panels, sew the panels for each curtain together with a ½" seam. Hem the side edges and the bottom. Turn the top edge under enough to allow for the diameter of your curtain rod plus ½" for hemming. Either stitch the hem exactly the width necessary to fit the curtain rod, or, if you wish to have a heading, hem the top so that the hem stitching forms the top of the casing and a second line of stitching forms the bottom. If you wish to have rods in the bottom of the curtain too, make

casings in the top first, and then make the bottom. Careful measurement of the length will be needed to achieve a tight-fitting curtain.

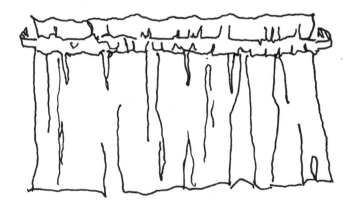

Fig. 16-8 *Casing Curtain*

117

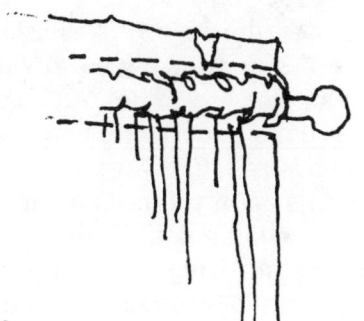

Fig. 16-9 *Casing Hems*

SHOWER CAP CURTAINS: Shower Cap Curtains are simple to make if you make a paper pattern first.

Step 1. Hold a piece of heavy paper up to the port you wish to cover. With a pencil, trace the outside edge of the port. Add to the paper pattern the depth of the port, from outside edge to cabin side. For instance, if the port protrudes 2″ out from the cabin side, extend the outline on the paper pattern 2″ all around. Add 1″ more for an outside ruffle (if desired) and ½″ for the hem. (With a 2″ port depth you would add a total of 3½″ to the original pattern outline.)

Step 2. Cut two pieces of fabric to fit the extended paper pattern. You can make the curtain reversible if you use a different fabric for each side.

Step 3. Place these two pieces right sides together, allowing a ½″ seam allowance, stitch around the outside, leaving the last 1″ open. Turn shower cap curtain right-side-out through opening left in seam.

Step 4. To make the outside ruffle, measure in 1″ from the outside edge and mark with a row of small dots all the way around the edge. Stitch along these dots, through both thicknesses, all the way around, leaving a small opening above the lower opening. Stitch again through both thicknesses ⅜" inch inside the first stitching line all the way around. If you have not added the extra 1" for a ruffled edge, make only one line of stitching ⅜" in from the outside edge.

Step 5. Measure and cut a length of ¼" elastic to fit snugly around the port. Allow an extra 1" for sewing the ends together. Fasten a safety pin through the end of the elastic, thread the elastic up through the first two openings and into the casing. Pull both ends out of the openings, overlap them 1" and stitch them together. Work the elastic around the casing so it is evenly distributed.

Step 6. Complete the outside casing stitching and close the hem opening. Stretch the elastic and place the shower cap over the port when privacy is desired.

NOTE: For a shower cap curtain *without* a ruffle, sew the second line of stitching (Step 4) ⅜" inside the outer edge all the way around, thread the elastic through (as in Step 5), and stitch outer hem closed.

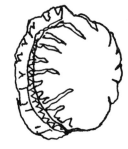

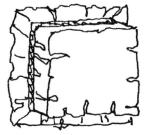

Fig. 16-10 *Shower Cap Curtain*

PLEATED CURTAINS

Pleats with Pleater Tape.

Pleater tape makes it easy to achieve uniform pinch pleats in a hurry. It will not always work on boats because boats often do not have the space between the top of the window and the overhead to accommodate the hardware needed to hang the drapes. Instructions are usually included with the tape, so we will not discuss it further here.

Pinch, Box and Cartridge Pleats

Pinch pleats, box pleats and cartridge pleats differ only in the manner in which they are folded. They are marked off on the fabric after the side and bottom edges of a curtain have been hemmed. A stiffener is required in the top hem to enable the pleats to stand stiff and straight. This stiffener or buckram can be purchased by the yard in different widths at most fabric stores. It is usually 4" wide which is fine for long drapes. Short pleated drapes, however, look better with a short pleat. If you cannot find the width you need, cut the 4" buckram down to the desired width.

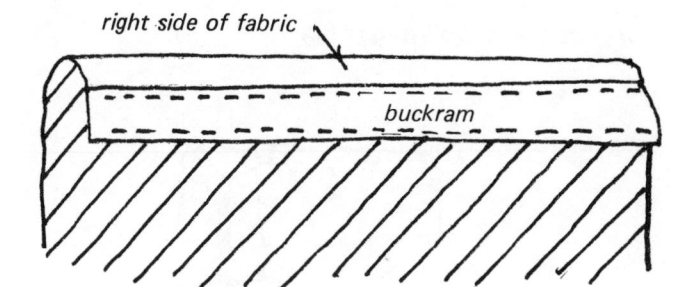

right side of fabric

buckram

Fig. 16-11 *Sewing in the Buckram*

Step 1. Lay the stiffener ½" over the top of the right side of the curtain. Stitch the stiffener to the drape close to the edge of the stiffener. Fold the stiffener to the wrong side of the curtain allowing ¼" of the fabric to show above the stiffener on the back side of the curtain. Press the stiffener and the top edge of the curtain flat.

Step 2. Press and hem the bottom and side edges of the curtain.

Step 3. Measure the width of the flat curtain and the width of the space you are going to cover. Subtract the space measurement from the curtain measurement to know how much cloth can be taken out with pleats.

Box pleats and pinch pleats need from 3" to 5" inches to be effective. Cartridge pleats usually use 2½" of cloth. Divide the width of each pleat or pleat allowance into the amount of cloth you have to take out. This will tell you how many pleats you can make. For example, you have a 60" flat curtain and a 20" window space. Your calculations go like this: i.e.:

window measurement is:	20"
3 × 20" = 60" of curtain.	
Subtract 20" from 60" to	60"
determine how much fabric to	−20"
remove with pleats.	40"
If a 5" pleat is used, divide	
40" by 5" to determine	40" ÷ 5" = 8"
the number of pleats needed	
to remove 40".	
If 8 pleats are needed there	
will be 9 spaces between the	
pleats. Divide the desired	
width of the curtain, 20" ÷ 9" = approx. 2¼"	
20", by 9 to determine between pleats	
the space between pleats.	

Mark the top of the drape on the stiffener with small dots to tell you where to make the pleats.

Step 4. Match the pleat dots on the stiffener and make a fold at the center of the pleat allowance. Stitch from the top of the curtain to about ½" below the stiffener. Backstitch both ends of this stitching line. Do this to all of the pleat allowances.

Step 5. Pinch pleats are made by folding the pleat allowances in thirds and hand-tacking or machine stitching the pleats together.

Box pleats are made by folding the pleat allowance flat against the pleat seam so that the folds are equidistant from the middle of the pleat and hand stitching both pleats ½" above the lower edge of the buckram.

Cartridge pleats are made by stuffing the pleat allowance with a rolled piece of stiffener or cotton batting.

LINING

Choose a lining that is preshrunk and sun resistant. Prepare the lining fabric the same way you prepared the curtain panels. Be sure to find the straight of the grain before cutting any panels.

121

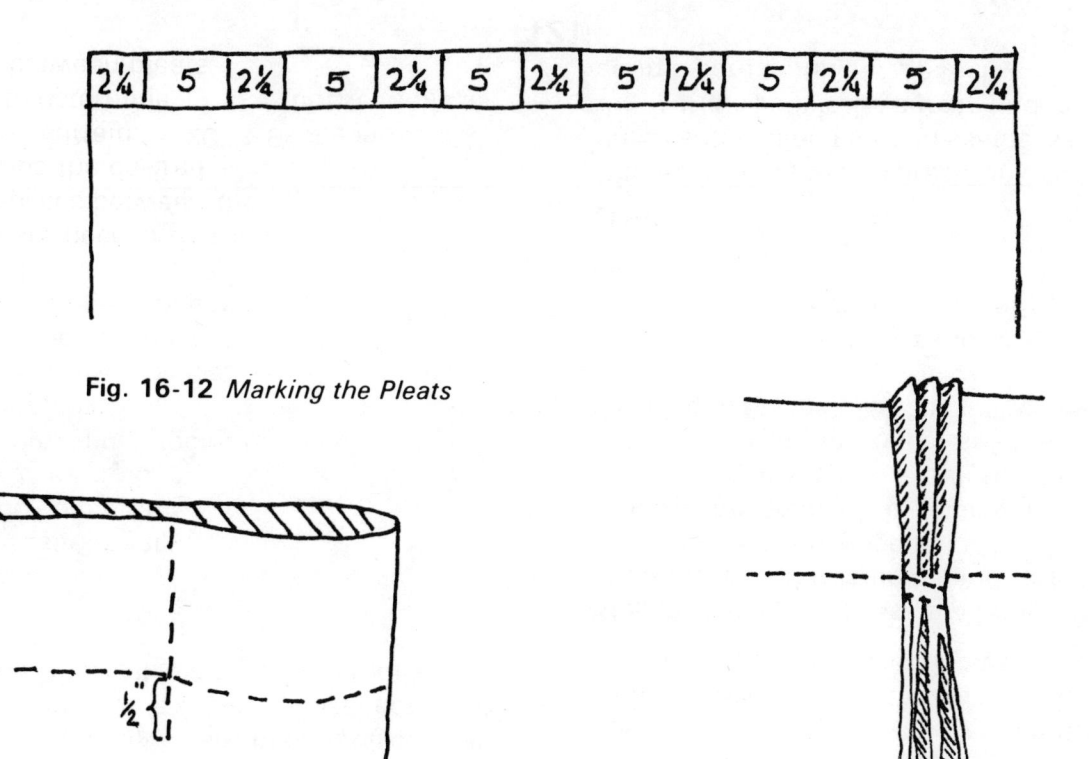

| 2¼ | 5 | 2¼ | 5 | 2¼ | 5 | 2¼ | 5 | 2¼ | 5 | 2¼ | 5 | 2¼ |

Fig. 16-12 *Marking the Pleats*

½"

Fig. 16-13 *Stitching the Seam Allowance*

Fig. 16-14 *Stitching a Pinch Pleat*

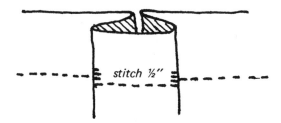

Fig. 16-15 *Stitching a Box Pleat*

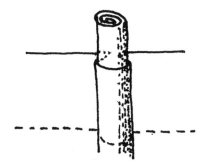

Fig. 16-16 *Stuffing a Cartridge Pleat*

Casing Curtains

Step 1. After sewing the necessary number of panels together for both the curtain and the lining, place them right sides together, and stitch the curtain and the lining panels across the top and sides. Turn right side out and press the panels flat.

Step 2. Hem the side edges with a 1" hem.

Step 3. Fold the top over, enough to make the casing for the top rod, and stitch. (Fig. 16-9)

Step 4. Finish the raw edge of the bottom by folding over a ¼" hem on both the curtain and the lining. Stitch these edges together. Make another line of stitching, the width of the rod, above the first line of stitching for the bottom casing. If there is no bottom rod, hem the curtain and the lining as discussed above.

Pleated Drapes

Step 1. After properly preparing the lining fabric, cut the panels needed 2" narrower and 1½" shorter than the corresponding curtain.

Step 2. Follow the instructions for pleated curtains, preparing the curtain as in Step 1.

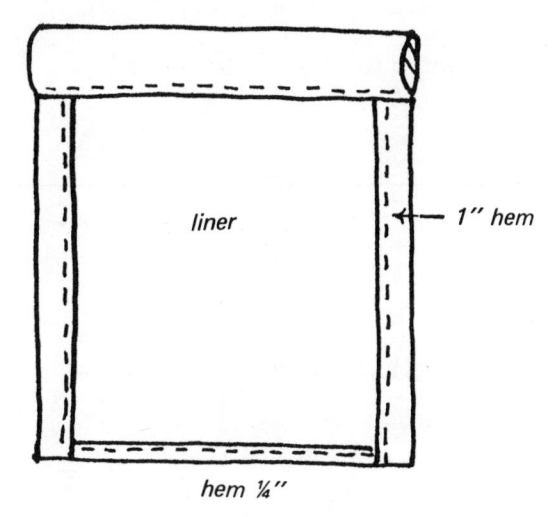

liner

← 1″ hem

hem ¼″

Fig. 16-17 *Lining a Casing Curtain*

with a ¼″ seam allowance. Turn right side out and center the lining over the curtain so that you have equal side hems. Press flat.

Step 6. Stitch the top folded edge of the lining to the curtain. Hem the lining and the curtain so that they

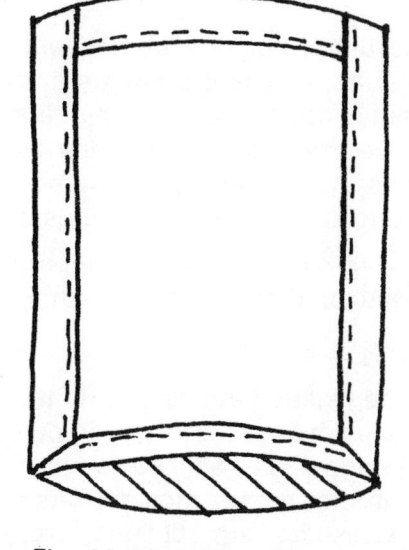

Fig. 16-18 *Lining a Pleated Drape*

Step 3. Hem the bottom of the curtain and the bottom of the lining.

Step 4. Press ¼″ of the top edge to the wrong side of the lining.

Step 5. Place the curtain and the lining right sides together so that the top folded edge of the lining is just a hair above the stiffener, and stitch the side seams

hang free of each other. The bottom corners of the curtain may need to be mitered to meet the hem of the lining. The lining should be approximately ¼″ shorter than the curtain. Mark and stitch the pleats as described in Steps 3, 4, and 5 under Pleated Curtains.

Pleats with Fasteners

Curtains that are fastened at the top and bottom with plastic slides can be pleated with the fastener.

Step 1. Prepare the curtain as you would a pleated drape but put 4″ of stiffener in the bottom as well as the top.

Step 2. Calculate the spacing of the plastic sliders so they will pleat attractively when the curtains are closed but not be too bulky when open. Mark the placement of the fasteners, being careful to keep the fasteners perfectly in line from top to bottom.

Step 3. Measure the exact distance between rods and transfer that distance to the curtain. Draw two lines, one across the top and the other across the bottom to indicate the exact placement of each fastener. Measure the exact width you wish the curtain to be when closed. Cut pieces of bias twill tape

exactly that length both for the top and bottom of the curtain.

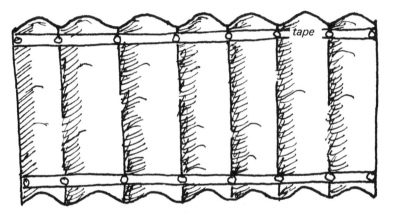

Fig. 16-19 *Pleating with Fasteners*

Step 4. Pin the bias tape to the curtain at the spots you have marked for fasteners. Begin by pinning each end of the tape to the side edges of the curtain. Next pin the middle of the tape to the middle-fastener spot. Then divide the right section in half and pin the fasteners in that section. Continue pinning the tape to

125

the fastener locations in this manner until you have all the pleats equally folded with pins. Tack the fastener and the tape to the curtain as you have pinned them. (Note: The tape is only sewn to the curtain under each fastener.)

Fig. 16-20 *Setting the Folds*

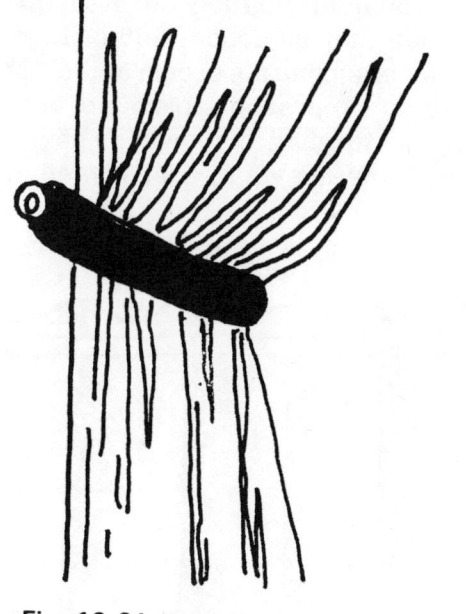

Fig. 16-21 *Tie-Backs*

Step 5. Hang the curtains by attaching a top fastener and then a bottom until the entire curtain is hung. Pleat the drape as it should be and tie open for a few days to set the pleats.

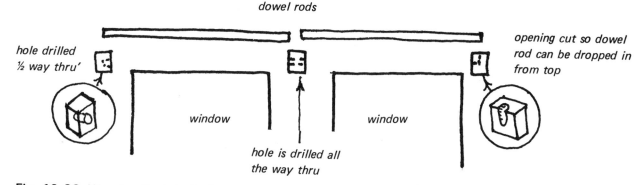

dowel rods

hole drilled
½ way thru'

opening cut so dowel
rod can be dropped in
from top

window

window

hole is drilled all
the way thru

Fig. 16-22 *Wooden Curtain Rods*

HANGING THE CURTAINS

All curtains look better after they have been hanging for a few days. You can help the curtains to hang well if you will spend a few minutes gathering each curtain on the rod and arranging the pleats or the folds. Once you are satisfied that they are hanging correctly, tie each panel to set the pleats.

TIE-BACKS

To make a tieback out of the same material as the drapes, measure the circumference of the drape as it hangs in its open position. Cut a length of cloth 1" longer than this measurement and 1" wider than you wish the tieback to be. Fold the strip of cloth in half, right sides together, and stitch one end and the open side edge. Turn the strip right-side-out and hem the open end. Press. Decorative cording can be stitched on the right side of the tieback if desired. Attach the tieback to the bulkhead or window casing with a male snap that is screwed through one end of the tieback and then into the window casing, and a female snap that is attached to the other end.

Tiebacks can also be made with spliced line, ribbon or trim braid.

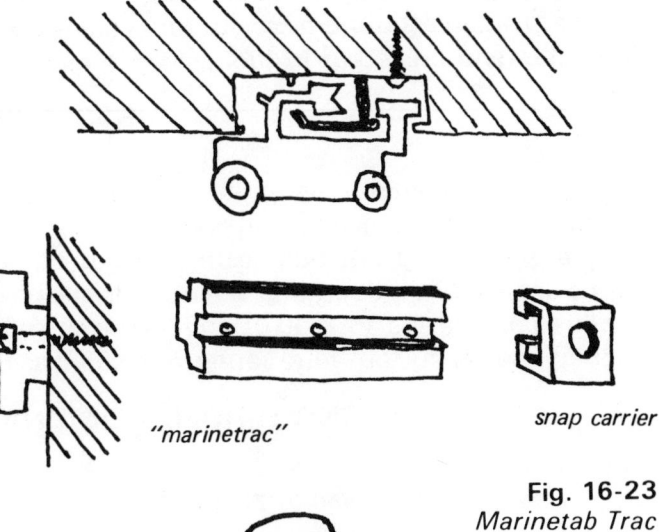

"marinetrac"

snap carrier

Fig. 16-23
Marinetab Trac

Fig. 16-24 *Sew-On Tab*

FASTENINGS AND HARDWARE

When you are choosing hardware for your curtains, take into consideration the type of drape you are hanging, where the curtains will fall, and where you must fasten the hardware. A simple drape that does not have to be pleated or full may be easily attached to a bulkhead with Velcro tape. Use contact cement to hold the softer strip to the bulkhead and sew the prickly side of the Velcro tape to the top of the curtain. This type of drape can be removed when not in use. Cafe curtain rods for casing curtains can be used on the top and bottom of a curtain, or you can make your own rods out of wooden blocks and dowels.

Whatever you use, *don't buy* hardware made of metal (ferrous) that will rust. Check it with a magnet if in doubt. Stick to brass, aluminum, plastic or stainless steel, or your curtains will be rust-stained in no time, especially in a salt-water atmosphere.

There are several different brands of hardware for hanging pleated drapes. Kirsch of Sturgis, Michigan, is the manufacturer of the system that is often installed in production boats but there are many others that are similar. Basically the system consists of a slotted track that is mounted on the overhead or the top of a window casement. Several different types of tabs are offered for attaching the drape to the track.

The snap carrier is used in combination with snap-on tape. This tape is used in the same manner as pleater tape and often has the pleat marks already stamped on the tape. If you wish to cut down on costs, use sew-on tabs. They are easily stitched to the top of the drape and don't tear easily. Be careful to place all the tabs at exactly the same level or your hem line will be thrown off.

When you buy Kirsch hardware, you get a table of measurements for making curtains with 60% fullness using the Kirsch snap-tape system. This table will work with the sew-on tabs, too, and you can increase the fullness if you wish.

When planning your curtains be sure to consider the safety aspect of their positioning. Power yachts with flying bridges often have curtains over the forward windows of the saloon because the owners never plan to use the inside steering station. However, the first squall that forces them below often makes them curse drapes that won't open easily. Remember that curtains near stoves, navigation instruments or engine controls can pose a hazard. Consider also that curtains which are not firmly fastened may interfere with safe handling of the vessel.

CONCLUSION

In our travels and cruising we have sewn many covers for boat owners and found most of them uninformed on the subject of canvas but eager to learn. Trying to help them with their particular customizing problems we have found ourselves repeating the same instructions again and again. We hope that the instructions and directions found here have given all our boating friends the means to make the fabric accessories they have needed and wanted for their boats. We also hope that they have enjoyed the hours at the sewing machine and taken pleasure from the practical and esthetic aspects of the projects they've completed.

If you, the reader, are slightly disappointed with your first efforts because they didn't turn out as well as you had imagined them, remember that we all have to begin somewhere; your next project will go easier and look better. Even if you chewed your nails, growled a lot and dumped the project into the lap of your spouse, we can assure you that you've learned something about canvas work. As a craft, it's centuries old, so you cannot acquire its skills overnight. Even a less-than-perfect job is probably usable long enough to justify the materials cost. Don't give up! Keep at it! The next project will surely be easier and better.

Possibly you became creative and sewed up a "number" all your own. If so, then we have been truly successful in our efforts to make it possible for every boat owner to understand the basics of canvas craftsmanship.

Karen and Bob Lipe

APPENDIX

SOURCES OF MATERIALS AND HARDWARE

Fabrics and supplies:

THE COVERLOFT, Inc.
726 Second St.
Annapolis, MD 21403

W. VALENTINE CO.
Div. of Jac Music Co. Inc.
618-622 S.W. 8th St.
Miami, FL 33130

TEXTILE COMMISSION INC.
217 Chestnut Street
Philadelphia, PA 19106

UNITED TEXTILE AND SUPPLY
795-61 North Spring St.
Los Angeles, CA 90012

THE ASTRUP CO.
945 W. Flagler St.
Miami, FL

HOWE AND BAINBRIDGE, Inc.
220 Commercial Street
Boston, MA 02109

Foam Rubber:

AMERICAN EXCELLSIOR CO.
Baltimore, MD

FLEXIBLE FOAM PRODUCTS DIV.
Box 5527, Great SW Sta.
Arlington, TX 76011

3500 N.W. 114th St.
Miami, FL 33167

1310 Atlantic St.
N. Kansas City, MO 64116

6610 Anderson Rd.
Tampa, FL 33614

6000 So. Oak Park Ave.
Chicago, ILL 60638

1506 First Ave.
Evansville, IN 47710

5700 So. 7th St.
Ralston, NB 68051

613 S. 4th St.
Elkhart, IN 46514

Fasteners:

TRW DOT DIVISION
P.O. Box 710
Waterbury, CT 06720

Upholstery fabrics can be purchased from local upholstery shops and fabric stores. Canvas supplies can also be purchased from your local sail loft.

ABOUT THE AUTHORS

Bob and Karen Lipe have lived aboard their 40-foot William Atkin ketch, *Errant,* for six years. They have cruised the Eastern Seaboard and the Bahama Islands for the past four years making canvas products for cruising people. They have an established reputation for nautical canvas work and have recently become the owners of a canvas loft.

Before buying *Errant* six years ago, Bob and Karen taught high school in Traverse City, Michigan, and sailed a 30-foot cutter on the Great Lakes. They have both been sailing since they were small children and, in fact, met one another at a Sailing Club meeting at Michigan State University where they went to school. They have written many articles for *Motor Boating* and *Sailing* Magazine, and expect to continue this free-lance writing as they cruise.

ABOUT THE ILLUSTRATOR

Jim Kraft was born and raised in Central Illinois and didn't know what a boat was until five years ago, when he moved to Elk Rapids, Michigan, on the eastern shore of Lake Michigan. Since then he has sailed avidly.

He is a teacher of Art at Traverse City High School and owns the Lure of the Lakes Gallery in Traverse City, Michigan, which specializes in nautical paintings, stained glass, enameled jewelry, and nautical gifts. He holds a B.A. in Art and a M.A. in Ceramics. His illustrations are a sample of his easygoing but persevering nature and we're glad to have him aboard.